KIRSTYN AUSTIN ^{AND} JANET FIFE-YEOMANS

INJUSTICE

KIRSTYN AUSTIN ^{AND} JANET FIFE-YEOMANS

INJUSTICE

RANDOM HOUSE
AUSTRALIA

Published by
Random House Australia Pty Ltd
20 Alfred Street, Milsons Point, NSW 2061
http://www.randomhouse.com.au

Sydney New York Toronto
London Auckland Johannesburg
and agencies throughout the world

First published 1998
Copyright © Kirstyn Austin and Janet Fife-Yeomans

National Library of Australia
Cataloguing-in-Publication Data

Austin, Kirstyn
  Injustice

  ISBN 0 091 83653 0

  Austin, Kirstyn. 2. Many, Fred. 3. Rape victims - New
  South Wales. 4. Trials (Rape) - New South Wales. 5.
  Threats - New South Wales. 6. Prisoners - New South Wales.
  Fife-Yeomans, Janet. II.Title.

36288309944

Design by Michael Killalea/Maxco
Typeset by Asset Typesetting Pty Ltd, Sydney
Printed by Griffin Press Pty Ltd

10 9 8 7 6 5 4 3 2 1

This book is dedicated to my Mum

You nursed me as an infant, you guided me as a teenager. My life took a turn but you took the turns with me. You also faced the battles when most wouldn't.

Your support, understanding and wisdom helped me through the insecure times and your love and laughter heightened the good times.

It's because of all these qualities and so much more that I've grown to become a woman of strength while maintaining compassion. I thank you from the bottom of my heart.

I love you.

ACKNOWLEDGEMENTS

I would like to thank my family for all their love, support and encouragement. I also thank Janet Fife-Yeomans and David Hardaker for all their listening, for putting up with all those phone calls and for their friendship. I couldn't have done any of this without you, Janet.

There are many people who deserve my thanks for supporting me through the years: To Michael and Helen Upton, Brian and Rhonda Collis, Rick Ashton and Kerrie McDonald I say a thank you from my heart for all you have done. Special thanks to John, Grahame, John, Andrew, Megan and the rest of the SWOS team. Warmest thanks to the two best friends I have ever known, Alison and Baden—you guys have always been there for me and I love you both. To Rosemary and Tina, the words of encouragement helped me more than you will ever know. To Adam for absolutely everything during the early days. To Richard Carleton, Cliff Neville and Howard Sacre for showing such compassion during my time in London. To Terry for your friendship and support and the occasional kick up the rear.

Finally to the two most important men in my life. Paddy, you've taken on an enormous amount coming into a relationship with me and yet you have handled everything with such ease and even had the ability to keep me sane and not let me get too dragged down by everything. I love you and couldn't imagine doing this without you.

To my darling Ben, you are growing into a beautiful young man with a heart as big as your eyes. You have made everything worthwhile.

Thank you to all of you.

K.A.

There are some special people without whom this book would never have been written. Many of them Kirstyn has already thanked. Some whose contributions have helped us piece together what went on behind the scenes with absolute accuracy have asked that they remain anonymous because of the jobs they hold. They will know who they are and deserve our gratitude. Others who have been closely involved with this story over the years and who have been generous with their time include Lyndie Cashman, who has never been too busy to help in the interests of accuracy and to whom I am very grateful. I remember well the day I first met Kirstyn and her mum through my work as a reporter covering Sydney's courts. I was struck by their warmth and their sense of humour in what could not have been worse circumstances. Few people could have come through this and maintained those important attributes. I am honoured that they have shared that warmth and their laughter with me, throughout all those long distance phone calls and now closer to home.

Special thanks go to my husband, David.

J.F-Y.

CONTENTS

PREFACE

When the phone rings in the middle of the night you know it's going to be bad news. The ringing woke me in the ground floor flat where I was living, I was up and out of bed and across the room in a flash to pick it up. It was Mum back home in Queensland and I had been right. It was the news I never wanted to hear.

It had been eight years and six months since I got into the car that summer day with the stranger who attacked me, raped me and left me for dead. The stranger was Fred Many. Now he was getting out of gaol, she said, on Saturday, 4 March 1995, just a few days away.

While he was about to leave his prison behind, I have carried mine around with me in my mind every day since the attack. At the time Mum made that call, I had been living overseas for four years. Fleeing Australia was the only way I could feel safe after Fred Many put out a contract on my life and on Mum's life. Since Easter 1987, Mum and I lived in the netherworld of witness protection. Mum stayed behind in Australia and I tried to find my peace in London. It was a city where I arrived on a one-way ticket knowing not a soul, on a passport which did not even bear my own name. I had said goodbye to the real me when I was given a new identity by the witness protection people. They had seen it as the only way to save my life.

When I answered the phone, I was thrilled to hear Mum's voice. Contact between us had been minimal since I moved because of the cost of telephone calls. It was really hard on us both because we had been through so much together and we missed each other desperately. She had not even seen her grandson, Ben, who was then a typical boisterous two-year-old. I had been looking for some kind of stability when I got married not long after arriving in London. As it turned out, I didn't wait long enough. My marriage was riddled with problems but at least I had my wonderful little boy. Although I had run all the way to the other side of the world, I couldn't escape my past. Yet again, it had come back to haunt me.

I had known, of course, that Many was due to get out of prison but I had put the exact date out of my mind. What hurt, what really hurt, was that he had been sentenced to spend twenty years in gaol for attacking me but the term had been cut by the judges on the New South Wales Court of Criminal Appeal to just eight years six months. He should have been behind bars until September 2006 but he received his reward for becoming a prison informer and informing on his fellow inmates. They might as well have given him a 'Get out of gaol free' card because in none of those cases did the prosecution obtain a conviction that stood. In two cases Many admitted he had lied and in another he simply refused to appear in court and give evidence.

He should never even have been free to attack me in 1986. He still had seven years, two months and seven days left to serve for a catalogue of offences including armed robbery and heroin offences when he was released from gaol in July of that year. He had walked out of prison early after ostensibly saving the life of a gaol superintendent, a 'good deed' which turned out to be a devious plot he had cooked up with another prisoner. Within six weeks he had tried to abduct two little girls aged nine and ten and had attacked me when I was fifteen. The whole situation stank.

Mum told me that we weren't the only ones who thought that Many getting out of gaol early a second time was an unparalleled injustice. Back home there was a public outcry which had astonished her by its intensity. The way Fred Many had been able to so cunningly rort the system had made him public enemy number one. The public was disgusted such a thing could happen. Our story was headlines in the newspapers, it led the evening television news and dominated talkback radio.

It had also caused more than a few problems for the New South Wales Liberal Government. Unfortunately for them, 4 March was the date of the state election and Fred Many had become the biggest election issue. With hours to go before he was due to walk free, they had set up a special police taskforce with detectives working around the clock investigating yet more charges against him but they ran out of time. When the Liberals lost, part of the blame was laid at the feet of a government which had been unable to keep Many in gaol and evidence that the public had lost faith in the party's law and order policies.

While I was out of the country, Mum had been speaking for us both. She had made many newspaper, radio and television appearances. With her face and voice disguised because of the fears that remained for our safety, she had explained the double dealings that had gone on before, during and after our case and how Many had successfully managed to manipulate the system. I could tell as her voice kept breaking down over the telephone line that the pressure was taking its toll and I knew she was worried sick about Many's release although she was trying to be brave.

Mum explained she hadn't wanted to remind me that Many's release date was so close or about the media attention because she feared it would upset me to have it all resurface again. After all this time, Fred Many still had the capacity to manipulate my life. He was entering my private world and turning it upside down yet again. However the fact that the whole ordeal was being aired again was no surprise to me and I was grateful to the media for picking up on it and grateful to the public for taking a strong stand against Many's early release.

Leading the reporting in the media was Janet Fife-Yeomans, legal writer for the *Australian*. Mum and I met Janet in 1990 when she publicised the decision of the Court of Criminal Appeal to slash Many's sentence. Her interest in Many began in the late 1980s when she was reporting on the law courts in Sydney and noticed his name becoming increasingly familiar as the key crown witness in a series of trials. Mum and I liked Janet straight away. She came across as being very understanding and honest. If it had not been for her persistence in digging into Many's history and the background to these high profile trials, the true story about what went on would never have been revealed.

As for me, I had been known for years in the media only as 'Many's fifteen-year-old rape victim', becoming an unidentifiable shadowy figure in the newspapers and on the television news. I was full of anger at what Many had done to my family and the way the justice system had allowed him to do the things he had done to me and pretty much get away with it. I wanted to speak up for myself and not have to have Mum do it for me. I wanted the public to finally see me as a real person not some mythical being and to acknowledge what happened to me.

That is the reason I began writing this book—I felt very strongly that it was time for the truth and I was sick of hiding. I was a fifteen-year-old girl living an average suburban life when this man violently changed it forever. I sometimes think that had I been raped by anyone else it would have been easier to get my life back on track.

Through Many and the opportunities he was given to twist the legal system to suit himself, my life and Mum's life became tangled up in a world I had never known existed outside a movie plot. There were the death threats, corrupt police, prison informers, drugs, bribes and some of the heaviest criminals in the country.

Then, while I was working on the book, came the news that Many had died of a heart attack. I thought his death would set me free but it has presented me with a whole new set of problems. How can I tell people close to me that I am not who they think I am, that I have been living a lie with them because there have been very few people I could afford to trust? Can I get my real identity back?

I feel the whole story, including what became my extraordinary life in witness protection, needs to be told so this can never happen to another person. However by the end of the book, while you will hear some answers, you will probably be left with more questions. Will we ever know the real truth about who helped Many slip through all those loopholes and why he was able to do this? I doubt it, but at least by writing this book, both Janet Fife-Yeomans and myself are able to let people know what can happen when criminals like Many are given the chance to bend the system.

CHAPTER 1

THE STRANGER

The day that changed my life forever is as fresh in my mind as if it were only yesterday. I can remember every single, stark detail of Tuesday, 2 September 1986.

I opened my eyes to another glorious day on the New South Wales Central Coast. It was eight o'clock in the morning and the sky was a brilliant blue. From my bedroom window I could see the ocean, the sun reflecting off its surface as if it were covered in millions of small pieces of mirror. I washed my face and headed into the lounge room where the windows looked out over the ocean again. We were living in a fourth floor corner unit in a small block at The Entrance. The unit was modest but it had a glorious view out to North Entrance Beach from the balcony running off the lounge room where I found Mum this morning, sitting and sipping coffee.

My whole life revolved around my loving family, my wonderful friends and, of course, the beach. I guess you could say that life was just about perfect for this fifteen-year-old girl. Mum, Dad and I had moved up to the Central Coast four years earlier from Sydney and I was in Year 9 at Terrigal High School. We were living in the flat while we built a house high up in the hills behind Terrigal and I was happily settled into the area.

It was the second week of the school holidays and every day had become like a form of ritual. I would meet my girlfriend Susie at her place, a few minutes' walk from Terrigal. We'd walk into Terrigal, catch up with some more friends and head to the beach. The only drama we had to deal with was split ends in our hair.

'Morning, Mum,' I remember thinking how on earth could my mother look so good at that time of the day, casually dressed in a pair of clean pressed jeans and a crisp white shirt with not a hair out of place. All my friends adored my mum. She is the sort of woman who always opens her heart and arms to people, making them feel important and cared for. There was never a shortage of my friends sitting down and talking to Mum, asking her advice.

'Morning, darling, how did you sleep?'

I leaned over the small outdoor table, kissed her on the cheek and answered, 'Good but I'm still waking up!'

I walked back into the kitchen and poured myself a glass of orange juice. Mum followed me, put her arm around my shoulder and asked about my plans for the day. I told her that I planned to phone Susie and see what was happening.

'Well, don't plan anything very elaborate, will you, sweetheart. Your dad has the car today so we're limited in where we can go,' said Mum.

Susie and I arranged over the phone to meet at her house and then decide what to do with our day. I asked Mum if that was all right and she looked a bit disappointed. It was the second day of her annual leave and she had been planning to spend all this time with me doing the things the two of us missed when she was working—like cooking favourite meals, baking scones and cookies and going for walks along the beach. Just the two of us. But typical of Mum, she didn't want me to feel guilty so all she did was groan and remind me again that she didn't have the car. She asked if Susie could come to our place instead but I moaned at Mum, saying how much better it was spending the day at Terrigal because all my friends from school were there.

'I know you prefer it, baby, but I just don't like the idea of you going all that way on the bus by yourself,' she said.

I pleaded with Mum, promising I would be careful and ring her as soon as I got to Susie's. Eventually she relented. She sat me down and made me promise I wouldn't talk to anyone and that I'd be careful.

I said, 'I will, Mum, you know I will.'

Mum still wasn't happy about the idea but I think she gave in knowing that having me hanging around the flat all day sulking would drive her mad.

I raced into my bedroom and packed my knapsack for the day. It had been my birthday a few weeks earlier and I had some new clothes I wanted to show Susie, so into the knapsack they went along with a jumper in case the weather changed, a towel, sunscreen, hairbrush and my purse. By the time I had finished, the knapsack felt as if it had been packed for a week away.

Mum made sure I had plenty of money for the return bus fare and we arranged that I would be home by 4.30 p.m. It was 11 o'clock when I kissed her goodbye and headed off. I always took the shortcut to the bus stop— across the car park behind the shops in the main street of The Entrance. Just as I was about to cross the street, I turned and looked back at the balcony that came off Mum and Dad's bedroom. Sure enough, there was Mum waving madly. She blew me a kiss before tapping her watch, letting me know not to forget the time I had to be home. I smiled to myself, thinking what a worrier she was.

I bought a can of coke as I waited for the bus. When the bus appeared I was happy to see the driver was Steve, the same driver who took me to school every day. He greeted me with 'Hi' as I took my usual seat right at the front of the bus next to the door and we chatted away. I always had a giggle to myself when I saw him because Steve was quite young with that typical surfie look; the tanned skin, slightly scruffy blond hair. All the girls had crushes on him, of which he seemed totally unaware, which only made it worse because he could chat in a really friendly manner that made them all swoon. Of course, I'd be lying myself if I said I was totally unaffected by his looks and his casual manner. Then again, at that age we all had posters of Wham! on our bedroom walls, Princess Di was our hero and we thought she should be Queen.

It took the bus about twenty minutes to reach my stop at Wamberal, the same stop I got off at on my way to school.

'Say hi to your Dad for me,' Steve called as I jumped from the bus and started on the long walk into Terrigal. This was the only drawback of going to Susie's place, a thirty-minute walk and it was already starting to get hot. I took the back streets which led from The Entrance Road down to Ocean View Drive, past a small park where as usual there were some little children playing under the ever watchful eyes of their parents. The knapsack on my back felt like it had tripled its weight when I heard a car horn sound behind me and a car pulled over to my side of the road. I was cautious at first because I didn't recognise the car. I leaned forward slightly towards the car to look closer but then a friend from school, Carmel, jumped out and asked if I wanted a lift into Terrigal. I gave a sigh of relief and accepted gratefully. She introduced me to her mum as I climbed in and we chatted non-stop all the way into town, catching up on the latest gossip. As we pulled up in front of the Cobb and Co Motel on Terrigal Drive, I thanked Carmel's mum for the lift and walked the last ten minutes to Susie's house.

Susie had been watching for me and had the door open before I even had the chance to knock.

'You're early, how come?' she asked.

I told her about the lift from Carmel's mum and then rang my mum just like I'd promised to let her know I had arrived safely. She was relieved and said she'd see me later. We ended the conversation with us both saying 'I love you' and hung up.

Then Susie and I set about pulling my clothes from my knapsack and trying them on. We had a laugh about some of the looks we achieved when we added some bits and pieces from Susie's wardrobe and ended up looking like something out of a bag full of rags. We changed back into gear that wouldn't scare half the population and headed into Terrigal to see what was happening.

A stiff breeze had come up off the ocean and the perfect blue sky was dotted with clouds. We hoped it didn't mean rain—the weather always changed so quickly on the coast.

We sat in our usual spot on the small brick wall which surrounded a small garden set into the footpath opposite the video arcade. All the kids in the area hung out around the arcade, it was the recognised meeting place for us all. Terrigal as usual was a hive of activity, locals rushing around and tourists everywhere.

Cathy, the third girl who made up our trio, turned up. The three of us went everywhere together and were rarely seen apart.

'So what's up?' she asked.

'I don't know, what do you feel like doing?' I replied.

The three of us looked at each other and shrugged our shoulders. This was life on the coast. It was such a laid-back place that the day-to-day activities soon took on a slight boredom factor.

Reluctantly we moved away from our seats and immediately other young people parked themselves there. We wandered off around the shops, stopping in at Perry's milkbar, another of our haunts, before continuing on our mission of finding something to do.

Halfway along the main street was a large chemist shop.

'Hey girls, let's go in here and have a look,' said Susie.

Susie was always after something in the chemist's. She was the only girl I knew who had a selection of eight different sunblocks, even more face creams, make-up … you name it, she had them all. I figured this would be fun.

We headed straight for the sale table where we tried out the different coloured zinc creams until we looked like walking rainbows. Then I spotted some false nails. I had always fancied trying some, I thought they looked pretty glamorous, and Susie and Cathy helped me pick out some that didn't look too much like talons. Then they helped me pick out some nail varnish. We were all attracted to the colours that were the most striking, the bright pink, the vibrant orange. I very nearly chose the pink but stopped myself, knowing Dad would have a fit about the false nails alone let alone some shocking nail polish. I knew the bright pink would just see me grounded for the rest of the holidays. I ended up with a soft pinky-blue mother of pearl colour, much to the annoyance of the girls.

Back at Susie's house, the whole messy process of putting on my nails seemed to take forever. Susie was playing around with the ones I didn't use, pretending to stick them on her toes. Cathy and I christened her Godzilla. Once my nails were fixed and painted, I admit I thought they looked pretty good. It was two o'clock by then and the girls wanted to go to the beach but I reminded them I only had an hour and a half before I had to leave to get home on time. We decided to go to Wamberal Beach which was the halfway point for me on the walk to the bus stop. It meant I only had to walk part of the way by myself.

I heaved my knapsack back on to my shoulders and in no time we were on the sand. It's always like that, time just flies when you're walking and talking with friends. The breeze had picked up so we wimped out of going for a swim, choosing instead to sit along the side of Wamberal Surf Club in a lovely sheltered spot which proved to be both a great windbreak and sun trap. It faced west and we lifted our faces up to the sun. All the walking I'd done that day had tired me out.

I thought about the situation at home. Our move up to the Central Coast was meant to bring Mum and Dad closer together after they had separated for a short period, but it was not working. The only thing that marred my near perfect life was that they were still arguing and I was finding it harder and harder to remain hopeful that things would calm down and we could all get back to normal. Mum has always been such a loving person and emotionally so soft that she would be in tears every time she had a row with Dad. Mum and I had always been very close and although I loved Dad, he didn't show much affection. Dad had been raised by a strict father and his mother had died during an asthma attack when he was young and I think that must have had a lot to do with it. On one hand I wished so much that the two of them could work it out while on the other hand I wished they would split up so the three of us could get on with our lives.

Dad had his own business, manufacturing kitchens, and since we had moved to The Entrance, Mum had been working two jobs to pay for the building of the new house. She would be away from home every morning by 7.30 for her day job, as a receptionist at a doctor's surgery. She was adored by all the patients and I know that was what kept her going when she got tired. No sooner would Mum come home, quickly have something to eat than she would be out the door rushing to her night job, as a receptionist at a local recreational club.

Thankfully she got a job as a receptionist at a Sydney commercial radio station. The travel was hard as she had to catch the bus to Gosford, the train to Sydney and then a fifteen-minute walk to the radio station. The money was not much more than she was getting with the other two jobs—but she loved the work and the people. Of course, I thought it was all very glamorous and exciting because of the stature of the on-air personalities she got to meet, like John Laws and Mike Carlton.

I dragged myself away from my thoughts, making a mental note to give Mum a big hug and kiss when I got home. Speaking of home, I looked down at my watch and saw it was 3.30 p.m. Time to go.

'I'm going to have to go now, you two.' I left Susie and Cathy lying there in the sun with their eyes closed, leaning against a bench seat.

Susie asked if I wanted them to walk up to the main road with me but they looked too comfortable to move. Anyway, I knew I'd be all right.

'See you later,' we called to each other.

I turned and waved as I headed up to Ocean View Drive and turned right towards the bus stop. Once away from the beach, the breeze dropped and the sun seemed to get hotter. Soon I was sweating and wishing I'd stayed with Susie and Cathy at least until the sun dropped a little and things cooled down. Mental note number two, ask Mum if I could get home later next time. I crossed over to walk on the left-hand side. There was a better view of the ocean from this side and the houses had been built up high to take advantage of it. The houses also provided long shadows which just covered me. If I stayed close to their front fence line, I could just manage to keep out of the sun.

I was thinking about the long cool shower I would have when I got home when I heard a car pull up behind me. Thinking nothing of it, I kept walking. I was grumbling to myself about how hot and sticky I felt in my white leggings. Mum had bought them for herself but I had wanted to wear them today. At the time, it had seemed like a good idea but I had no idea how hot they would make me feel. I had my yellow one-piece swimming costume on underneath and a pink T-shirt over the top.

I could still hear the car behind me and I turned my head slightly to see what was happening. There was a white sedan crawling along by the kerb. I turned around further and looked back over my shoulder, thinking that perhaps the car was waiting to turn into a driveway and I was in the way. However I saw the car wasn't indicating that it planned to turn so I kept on walking. I'd only gone a short way from Dover Road and was just past Wiles Avenue, which headed off to the right when the car sped up a little and pulled into the kerb about three metres ahead of me. I wasn't really thinking much about it. I assumed it was a tourist. Then a movement caught my eye and I looked across into the car. There was a man in the driver's seat leaning across to the passenger side. I was still walking in the shadow close to the fence line as I looked at him. He had full, wavy hair, a mousey brown colour, just brushing his collar. His right hand was hanging over the top of the steering wheel and his left hand was on the back of the passenger seat, supporting his weight as he leaned over. His shoulders and arms looked huge and I thought he must be into a sport of some kind. He was wearing a light-coloured shirt and the impression I got was that he looked a little unkempt, sort of messy. His jaw looked like a triangle hanging off his face in a comical sort of way. But his eyes were what stood out the most. I could see they were light-coloured and they seemed to bore into me. It was a little unsettling.

He leaned over a little more and motioned with his left hand for me to come over to his car. BANG! Everything my family had told me about talking to strangers flashed through my mind at an incredible rate—Mum nagging at me about the dangers, about all the sick and twisted people out there in the world, always talking to me about the dreadful stories that would appear on the evening news. I recalled how recently a nine-year-old girl, Samantha Knight, had gone missing in Sydney. But that was Sydney, nothing ever happened up here on the coast. I didn't dwell much on Mum's warnings, believing the man had lost his way and needed directions. I smiled and walked over to his car. I did look around to see if anyone was around. I don't know why, it was almost subconscious. I couldn't see anyone out in the street but I could hear the sound of a lawnmower nearby. I leaned down and looked into the car through the open passenger window. I smiled, said 'Hello' and waited, still thinking he was going to ask directions.

'G'day,' he said and smiled back. 'Wanna lift, love?'

'Oh, I thought you needed directions,' I replied.

'No, love, I know where I'm going. I just thought it's a hot day and you look like you could use a lift. Are you headed far?' he asked.

I was surprised at being offered a lift by a complete stranger.

'Um, oh no, I'm fine. I'm only going up to the bus stop on the main road but thanks anyway,' I said. I straightened up, ready to start the long walk up the hill to the bus stop when he spoke again.

'Are you sure? You look pretty tired and I'm going that way anyway, right past it in fact,' he said.

I turned back and looked at him again and this time I noticed a wedding ring on his left hand. Feeling myself relax, I thought 'How lucky can one girl be? A lift from Carmel's mum this morning and now a chance of another lift. Mum will be surprised to see me home early for a change.'

So with all the innocence of a fifteen-year-old girl in that spring of 1986, I smiled and said: 'Thanks very much. I am feeling pretty hot and tired.'

With that, I opened the front passenger door, climbed into the car and sat down on the seat.

The sun was streaming through the windscreen and I could still hear the waves crashing on the shore down on Wamberal Beach. Everything seemed perfectly normal and calm. As I leaned forward to put my knapsack on the floor by my feet, the man reached over behind me and locked the door. It was an older-model car and still had the push-down button locks at the base of the windows on the top of the door vinyl. I thought it an odd thing to do and looked at him.

He smiled back. 'Better to be safe,' he said.

As we were about to pull away from the kerb, he turned and told me, 'Put your belt on, love.'

I didn't think anything was strange about this because Mum and Dad wouldn't go anywhere unless we all had our seatbelts on. I did as he asked, noticing as I turned my shoulder slightly to the left to pull the belt across my body just how dirty and dusty his car was. It was a real mess. There were papers strewn all over the floor and the small shelf beneath the glovebox had papers and food wrappers stuffed into it next to a red first aid box. There was also something that appeared to be a small cane box. I couldn't tell exactly what it could have been used for but I had seen nothing like it before.

We pulled away from the kerb and headed up the slight hill of Ocean View Drive which came out on The Entrance Road. I was looking out of the passenger window, feeling a little unsure of what was the appropriate thing to say to a stranger in their car. I turned my head towards him and said, 'Thanks very much for the lift. To be honest, I wasn't looking forward to the walk.'

He didn't reply and I got the impression that he wasn't a talker so I sat quietly and waited as we neared the bus stop. We reached the end of Ocean View Drive and I expected him to turn right towards The Entrance and my bus stop. I was surprised when I saw he was turning the car left but then realised there was another bus stop on the left side as well and I thought he must have assumed I had meant that was the one I wanted. It didn't worry me that we were heading in the wrong direction because by getting out at this bus stop, it meant I only had to cross the road and walk all of two minutes to the bus stop I wanted. I wasn't concerned at all. I leaned forward and gathered up my knapsack. I sat back and looked out of the windscreen at the bus stop about twenty metres ahead of us.

'Just here would be great, thanks,' I said happily.

There was no-one waiting at the bus stop which must have meant I'd missed the bus but at that time of the day the buses ran every thirty minutes so I knew I wouldn't have long to wait for the next one. But the car wasn't slowing down as I expected it to.

'If I could get out here, thanks. This is the bus stop I need,' I said.

I was surprised to hear the urgency in my voice and by this stage, the hairs on the back of my neck had risen. I waited for him to indicate and pull over to the left and when he made no attempt to do this, I was about to yell at him to stop the car. Before I could open my mouth again, he glanced at me and all I saw was a snarl come to his lips and a flash of movement. Then I felt a burning sting across the left side of my face. It took a split second for me to realise he had slapped me.

CHAPTER 2

THE LIFT

The sun was still streaming through the windscreen. I was alone in a strange car with a man I didn't know who wouldn't stop the car and who had just slapped me across the face. It felt like it took forever for the realisation of what was happening to sink in but in reality, it would have been only a few seconds. I suffered the most acute fear I had ever felt. My first thought was: 'Why me?' I wished I could have rewound the last thirty minutes of my life and wiped out one second's mistake of getting in this car. My next thought was: 'What do I do? How can I get away from this man?'

I could feel myself shaking all over. I could almost hear the blood draining from my body. It felt as if there was a huge dark hole beneath me and all the blood was sinking into it, leaving me icy-cold. More questions flooded through my mind. What does he want? Why is he doing this? What have I done? God, I prayed, just give me my mum and dad, please give me back my safety. I burst into uncontrollable tears of fear.

'What do you want?' I sobbed.

He was deadly calm, not nervous, not jittery. It was like he had it all planned. He looked at me and this time I was struck by the cold, hard look in his eyes.

'Shut up, nothing is going to happen to you so just stop your whimpering,' he said, in a way that was commanding and in control.

Yet his words of reassurance had a false ring to them and they did nothing to quell my terror. I knew I had entered a situation from which I wasn't sure I would walk away. My heart was racing, my body shaking and my eyes were stinging with tears. I ran my tongue along the inside of my mouth and tasted the blood that was seeping from the jagged edges of the inside of my cheek. When he had hit me, my teeth had caught the inside of my cheek and also cut my tongue. I could already feel the left side of my mouth swelling up.

We were still heading along The Entrance Road towards Gosford and outside the sun was still shining but all of a sudden, the beautiful day that had started out so sunny and warm felt as if it had been hit by a cyclone. Everything was being thrown around and twisted into the form of the man sitting next to me. Inside the car it was cold, cold and evil. I felt as if I was the focus of this evil. I knew I had to gather my senses. I had to work out a way to get myself out of this. I felt as if it was happening to someone else and that I was looking on, still with a sound mind and able to think logically. I tried to calm down and suppress my crying. Wiping my nose with the back of my hand, I turned to him.

'Look, please don't hurt me. I'm sorry if I've done something wrong, please don't hit me. My dad hits me all the time. He will beat me if he knew I had got into your car. I only did it to try to make him happy by getting home on time. Please, please let me go,' I begged.

Of course Dad had never beaten me but I was desperately trying to talk my way out of this man's car and the only thing I could think of was to try to make him see me as a victim already and maybe even appeal to his good side. I thought I had succeeded. I could have sworn I saw his face soften a touch. I am sure he even smiled a little. But whatever it was came and went in a flash.

Then another plan came to me. Perhaps if I could get him to slow down a little, I could open the car door and jump out. I waited a few minutes and then started to increase the sound of my breathing. With my chest heaving, I brought my hand up and clutched at my chest. Leaning forward a little, I tried to make my breathing sound uneven and stilted. I glanced across to see if he had noticed and thank God, he was looking at me while still trying to watch the road. I threw my right hand out and motioned to him with my fingers that I couldn't breathe.

'Asthma,' I gasped and made a choking noise. I was readying myself to jump from the car by turning myself inch by inch to my left to unlock the door and escape.

I thought I had succeeded in worrying him when I felt the car slow down. In my relief, I let my breath return to normal, losing all concentration on what I was doing and betraying myself as I anticipated my freedom. That error cost me dearly. He was not to be fooled. I felt a vice-like grip on my right shoulder and he forced me round to sit up straight, facing the windscreen again.

'No, you don't,' he said, emphasising each word and he laughed.

I knew now that anything I said would be futile. He had no intention of letting me out and I was scared that if I persisted in trying to get away from him, it would make things worse.

I figured talk was no good and it was action that was needed. It was just after four o'clock by this time and the traffic was building up as people drove home from work. It seemed as if the lives they were living were suddenly alien to me, locked in the capsule of this car. I felt they should be able to feel my fear but they drove past without a glance at us. I had an idea for what I thought would be a last attempt to get away—if we were to have an accident and I ran, he couldn't chase me without people seeing and I would certainly have an opportunity to run into a shop or a house to get help.

My plan was to reach across him, grab the steering wheel and try to ram us into another car or pole, anything that would cause a commotion and give me a chance to run. I started to prepare myself watching and waiting for the right moment, a time when we would slow down for a turning car or for a build-up of cars. Then the moment came. About four cars ahead of us, a car was waiting to turn right and we all had to slow down to pass on the inside lane. I tensed myself, getting ready to lean over and grab the wheel when a car passed us and in the back I saw a baby in a restraint. Then and there my plan died. I pictured a car wreck with a mother crying over her injured baby. How could I go ahead with my plan? Sure it would give me a chance to get away from this man, but at what price to others? I couldn't run the risk of serious harm to an innocent passerby through my own stupidity for getting into the car with a stranger.

My tears had stopped although my mouth kept skewing in that way it does when you try to stop yourself crying. My thought now was what was this man going to do? Not knowing was the hardest part, wondering what the outcome of this would be for me. I know now that the feeling I had that this was all unreal, that it was happening in another world, was brought on by shock. I was having the most diverse thoughts about my friends and family. I wondered not only if I would ever see them again but also what the last thing was that I had talked to each of them about. I tried to recall when the last family get-together had been and whether I had recently told the people who were so important to me that I loved them.

My reaction was like that feeling you get when someone creeps up behind you and grabs you. The automatic response is to jump, but then you find it takes a minute or two to calm your heart rate, to slow down the adrenalin. That original sharp intake of breath without the calming down that usually follows is how I felt the whole time I was with this man.

I felt a pain in each of my hands and looked down to find that I had been wringing them with so much force it had left red marks across each of them. I looked up and saw we had reached the Erina end of The Entrance Road. Something glinted and caught my eye and I looked down to see the sun was reflecting off some writing on the glovebox. The word 'Galant' was spelt out on it in silver letters. It was a make of car I had never heard of before but one which I would never forget. I looked back down to my hands and noticed that the seat I was sitting on was covered with a pale blue and green crocheted blanket. Suddenly the man spoke to me.

'So, have you got a boyfriend?' he asked.

I thought it an odd thing to ask but hoped that perhaps his concern was that there would be someone looking out for me. Although I didn't have a boyfriend, I told him I did. Then he asked me if I had slept with him. Immediately, I regretted lying about having a boyfriend. I answered a firm, 'No.'

His next question sent a shiver through me.

'Have you ever screwed or are you still a virgin?' he said.

Why was he asking this? I turned and looked at him.

'No, I'm still a virgin,' I said firmly.

I didn't realise it then but my answer to that question would end any last chance I may have had of ever getting away.

'So what's your name anyway?' he wanted to know.

I was just about to tell him the truth when I quickly thought to change my mind. I told him my name was Sarah. I didn't ask him his name—I didn't want to know anything about him. I wanted no connections with him. He then asked my age and again I decided against telling the truth. I told him I was fourteen, hoping that by having him believe I was younger it would make him think twice about whatever he had in mind for me. His next words brought a glimmer of hope I had not dared think I would have.

'I didn't realise you were that young. I'll take you back to where you wanted to go,' he said.

The relief that surged through me was so great I felt weightless. I allowed myself a great sigh and could only envisage getting home and running into Mum's arms and sinking into the feeling of being safe. I promised myself never to do this again and to warn all of my friends against accepting lifts from people they didn't know.

By now we had reached a roundabout and turned left into Terrigal Drive. I knew this road would take me right past school and then past Susie's house. I thought I would ask to be let out between the two, so I could walk down the back streets to Susie's and he wouldn't see where I went. I didn't want him to know anything about me or my friends. I planned to tell Susie's mum what had happened and she would be able to drive me home.

As we neared the school, I thought: 'Not long now. I'll soon be safe.'

I had started to believe it.

Then I felt the car slow down and saw he was indicating to turn right. I realised this would take us alongside the school and in the opposite direction to where I had hoped we were going. My heart started to race again and I knew the nightmare wasn't over yet. I felt my body stiffen and panic reached out to my every bone. I broke out in a sweat.

'Where are we going? What are you doing? You said you were going to let me go,' I said.

Without looking at me, he replied, 'Mmm, but first you are going to do something for me.'

Everything in me died. I seemed to lose all emotion and my body slumped in the seat. I realised there was no getting away from him.

'Before I let you go, I want you to suck my cock,' he said calmly.

The bile rose in my throat and I had to battle to keep it down. I was shaking all over and I started crying again as the realisation of what was to happen to me sank in. I fought to get any words out.

'No, please, I can't. I won't. I've never done that before, please don't make me.' I was sobbing so hard my body was shaking violently.

'Oh come on, you look like you could give a good head job,' he said, leaning over and patting my knee.

If someone had given me a knife right then, I would have cut off the leg that he touched. I felt so sick, I just wanted to die. At the same time, something in me clicked and I made a vow to myself—I would do everything in my power to make sure he didn't get away with this. I began to memorise every street we went along, every turn we made, every detail about him and his car.

We had reached the Scenic Highway, a main road that runs from the back of Terrigal to Avoca Beach, and headed towards Kincumber, a rural area. At Kincumber, we took a left turn at a roundabout towards a seaside suburb called Copacabana. This part of the trip took about twenty minutes but seemed to rush past with bewildering speed. Throughout, the man said nothing, not a word. I wasn't sure whether this was a good sign or not. I didn't know what to make of what was going on. Then we drove to a bushy area I wasn't familiar with and I soon lost all bearing of where we were. In front of us was a steep hill with trees and shrubs on both sides. The car slowed down and came to a stop in the middle of the road. Then the man raised his left arm, and I shrank away from it, thinking he was going to hit me. But he raised his arm over my head and laid it across the back of the headrest of the passenger seat, looked back over his left shoulder and started to reverse into a driveway.

The driveway was concealed from the road by thick brush and trees. I saw there were three letterboxes and realised there must be houses along the drive, which wound away behind us and around to the right. I prayed a car would drive down that driveway and I would be able to cause a scene and get away. No-one came. What I remember the most after the man switched off the engine was the sound of the birds. It was deafening.

I was trying not to lose my mind as I waited for his next move. I turned away from him when I felt him grip the back of my neck with his left hand. It felt like a vice had been placed around my neck. It was then I realised his true strength. He started to pull me over to him and I grabbed for the car door, trying to pull myself away using my legs as leverage. His strength was too much for me. He pushed my head down towards his lap with one hand and I saw he was wearing football-type shorts. With his other hand, he had already pulled out his penis. My God, he is going to force me to do this, I thought. I have no choice. He forced my mouth over him and I tried to turn my head away. Then I felt a crack on the back of my head. He had punched me so hard I was sure he had used something other than his fist but he hadn't. He pushed my head down really hard as he mouthed obscenities and I felt his penis on my lips. I thought about biting it and then trying to get out the car and run away. But run where? I didn't know where I was and I didn't know how far away the nearest houses were along the driveway. If he caught up with me, I was sure he would beat me and kill me. I was too scared to stay but even more scared to take the risk and run.

He then put both hands on either side of my head and started pushing down again. I felt my lips being forced back against my teeth. Again he was telling me what he wanted me to do, calling me a bitch along with it. He had one hand on the back of my neck and grabbed a handful of my hair on the back of my head with the other. He pulled my hair really hard and pushed me back down. My lips started bleeding from being mashed against my teeth. Still grabbing my hair, he started to push down and lift up my head. I realised I was supposed to be moving up and down but I couldn't. I had never done this before and I wasn't going to do it now. I thought that if he wanted it, then he was going to have to do it himself. There was no way I was going to satisfy his sick needs voluntarily.

I couldn't stop crying and he was obviously angry that I wasn't doing what he wanted because he pulled my head up and flung me back across the passenger seat with so much force that my head slammed against the passenger window of the car. I sank down into myself and looked across at him, not knowing what to expect. Clutched in his left hand I saw several long strands of blonde hair, my hair. He had thrown me so violently that he had pulled some of my hair out. I turned to look out through the passenger window through my tears, brought the back of my hand up to my face and started to viciously wipe my mouth. I closed my eyes, trying to stop fresh tears and keep down the bile rising in my throat.

I heard a noise and felt movement in the car. My eyes sprang open and I prepared myself for another assault. I looked across and almost cried out— he was opening his door. This is it, I thought, he's going to let me go. I don't know where the hell I am but I don't care, he's letting me go. That was all I could think. Without saying a word, he got out of the car and walked around to the boot. He opened the boot and while he was fumbling about inside it, I thought I might have time to unlock my door and make a run for it. I no longer cared about the consequences of escaping from him. All I could think about was getting away. My split second of hope vanished as he looked over the top of the open boot into the car. He then held the boot lid down a little as he continued with whatever he was doing, keeping an eye on me at the same time. I knew as soon as I lifted the button to unlock the door that he would be there. Still, in the back of my mind I hoped he would let me go. How wrong I was.

Leaving the boot lid up, he walked to the passenger door and tried to open it. He had forgotten that he had locked the door when I first got in the car and yelled at me to hurry up, indicating he wanted me to open the door. For a moment I thought of locking all the doors and driving away but I had never driven a car before and had no idea how to do it. I looked at the ignition and saw he had taken the keys with him. He must have seen me glance at the ignition because he banged on the window with a fist. I did as he said, opened the door and held my breath. He yanked me out of the car by my arm and marched me around to the back. He steered me towards the boot, told me to get in and not make a sound. My legs turned to jelly and I was certain I was going to fall. All the fight drained out of me. It took what seemed like forever to get the strength to lift my leaden legs up into the boot. I nearly fell but he grabbed me and pushed me into the small space while yelling at me to hurry up.

I started to wish him dead.

He pushed me until I was lying down, bending my legs to fit in the boot. I curled up in a foetal position. I thought I was going to be sick and I started shaking uncontrollably again. He stood back looking at me and slowly closed the boot lid, closing off the outside world. Entombed in the darkness, I felt a terror I had never known before. The state of disbelief I had felt had long given way to the realisation that this was really happening and it was happening to me. I shivered as I felt the car shift with his weight as he got back into the driver's seat. The engine started and we pulled out of the driveway, bumping over the rutted road.

A small beam of light filtered into the boot and I looked for its source. There was a small gap between the lid and the body of the car near the left brake light where the lid didn't seal properly and I was able to see out and check where we were going. I saw we were heading back the way we had come and thought that perhaps he was taking me back to the spot where he had first approached me. Then he took a different turn. My eyes became accustomed to the dark and I could make out objects inside the dirty, dusty boot. I saw something shining and felt along the bottom towards it with my fingers. It was a piece of metal about thirteen centimetres long and two centimetres wide with a strip of tape along the top of it. I picked the metal up and prised it into the gap between the boot lid and the car, trying to pop the boot open but the metal wasn't strong enough. Desperate to do something, I manoeuvred myself on to my stomach and pushed upwards with my knees and arms, using all my strength to push backwards against the boot lid. Still the damn thing refused to budge. I turned myself back over and looked through the gap in the boot to see that we were indeed heading back the way we came. This time the thought that perhaps he planned to drop me off at Terrigal was only a fleeting hope—he had said he was going to let me go before and he hadn't.

We were driving along the Scenic Highway when a car behind began to draw closer to us. I could see a man driving and a woman sitting in the front passenger seat. I knew I had to try to get their attention. It was very noisy in the boot, as well as smelly from exhaust fumes, so I knew my shouts would be lost. Instead I managed to lift my left hand up and squeezed my fingers through the gap. I wiggled my fingers, making as much movement as possible, hoping the woman might see them and realise someone was locked in the boot. The left-hand indicator on our car started flashing, the light glowing inside the boot. I looked to see if the car behind us was indicating but it wasn't. In another attempt to attract their attention, I pushed my fingers further through the gap wincing with pain as the edge of the boot lid dug across my knuckles. As we turned, the other car continued straight on, the two people in it unaware of the fifteen-year-old girl in the boot of the car frantically trying to save herself. I realised the only person who could get me through this was me.

The dark boot felt like a coffin. I was struck by the thought that I might never walk away from this and if I disappeared, no-one would know what had happened to me. I knew Mum would already be on the phone to Susie asking where I was and I knew she would soon be driving along the bus route I always took home looking for me. I tried to keep a level head and think about what I could do to make sure there were at least some clues to me having been trapped in this car.

I noticed the back of the brake lights unscrewed, opening on to the light globes. I did think about undoing the globes so the police would notice there were no brake lights but figured this was a slim hope. I flicked my new false fingernails with the tip of my thumbs and then the idea came to me— I would rip them off and hide them in the brake light. In the dark of the boot, curled up in a tight ball, I pulled each fingernail off one by one—it must have hurt but I hardly noticed it—and pushed them into the left-hand brake light and screwed the back of the light back on. Then the thought of fingerprints came to me. In the books I had read and the television programmes I had seen, the police always seemed to use fingerprints to solve crimes. Above me was the boot lid so I rolled over on to my back and lifted up both hands, pressing my palms and the full length of each finger, including the tips, on the inside of the lid, hoping to leave a perfect set of prints for the police to find, hoping they would look for them.

The left-hand indicator was flashing again and we were turning into Terrigal Drive but heading away from Terrigal. I turned myself over and looked out through the gap of the boot. I could see there was another car behind us, although this one only had a driver . This time I picked up the strip of metal and slipped it through the gap along with my fingers. I wriggled my fingers and waved the metal, hoping the sun would reflect off it and catch the eye of the driver who would then spot my fingers. I almost screamed as I saw the car pulling back. It slowed down and made a right turn off our road. I quietly called out: 'No, no.'

Again the indicator light illuminated the inside of the boot and we turned into Duffy's Road. I felt the car slow down and stop, the door opened and I heard the man's footsteps approach. The boot lid sprang open and light came flooding into the space. He reached in and pulled me from the boot as I blinked my eyes, getting used to the brightness. Holding my breath, I waited to see if my legs would take my weight. He looked over my shoulder into the boot and for an instant I thought that somehow he knew I had done something and that he would find the nails inside the brake lights. But he pulled me roughly towards him, grabbing my left arm and dragging me to the passenger side of the car. Opening the door, he looked around and pushed me down into the seat. As he went to close the door, I looked up at him and said, 'I thought you said you would let me go?'

He got really angry, his face twisting up as he yelled, 'Just shut up.'

I could feel all hope draining away. I would just try to get through this without any unnecessary pain.

He locked the door and made me put my seatbelt back on. Again we headed back past my high school. I felt like he somehow knew this was insane torture for me, knowing I was looking on this area as my last link with safety and rubbing my nose in it. In deafening silence we drove on with me staring straight ahead. We reached the roundabout where we had earlier turned left towards Copacabana but this time around he made a right turn to Saratoga. There were cars everywhere but being surrounded by people just made me feel lonelier sitting here with this stranger. I knew I had no chance of doing anything to attract their attention. My brain felt heavy and I was exhausted from the constant fear and adrenalin that had gripped me during the last hour.

He headed into Saratoga and turned into a street that led along Brisbane Water. He seemed confident in this area and was manoeuvring the car with a casual ease. We took another right turn and drove past a small shopping complex. I could see families walking around and wanted so much to be with my family that my heart just ached for it. I felt so isolated watching how people were able to carry on doing their own, everyday things and have no clue about what was happening in this car that drove past them. He kept making turns and backtracking, Mumbling: 'This isn't right, this isn't it.' He seemed to be looking for something in particular.

Leaving his right hand on the wheel, he leaned across me and pulled the cane box from the shelf underneath the glovebox. I realised the cane box was used to keep cigarettes in. He flipped open the lid and took a cigarette out, putting it to his lips and lighting it with a lighter he kept in a matching cane box. Then he held the box out to me, offering me a cigarette. Like most teenagers, I had experimented with smoking but I wouldn't say I was a smoker. I accepted one because I wanted to see what brand he smoked—in the back of my mind was still the thought that if I did walk away from this, I wanted to give as much information as I could to the police. One thing was certain, I would make sure I did everything I could to stop him doing this to anyone else. The cigarettes he smoked were Peter Jackson in a blue box. At the same time I was puzzled as his attitude to me seemed to have changed yet again. His voice had lost its menacing tone. I didn't know what to make of it.

As we headed out of Saratoga and towards Gosford, I looked at my watch and saw it was 5.15 p.m.

'Um, I have to be home by 5.30 at the latest or Mum will be really worried and probably start looking for me. She's really protective and might even call the police,' I said to him, speaking quietly and even sounding apologetic, hoping he wouldn't get angry and think I was threatening him. He nodded his head.

'No worries, I'll have you back by then,' he said.

Although I allowed myself a glimmer of hope when he said he would have me back home soon, I knew by this time he was probably just saying it to keep me quiet and the urge to do everything I could to get away from him hit me again with a desperate force.

The traffic had built up, slowing to a crawl because of roadworks ahead. It was then I saw the police car about six cars ahead of us. Even though my thoughts were on escaping I was too scared to try anything in case I got myself into more trouble with him. My seatbelt was on, the passenger door locked and if I made even the slightest movement, his eyes snapped in my direction. The button to open the door was slightly behind me on the edge of the door. I would have had to turn right around to open it. There was no way I could do it without him stopping me. He knew what he was doing when he had me put my seatbelt on and, anyway, what could the officers in a police car do when they were way ahead of us? All I could do was sit and watch as it slowly pulled away.

We headed through Gosford without a word being said. My secret thought that he might let me out at the train station proved fruitless. He turned left before reaching the station and headed through West Gosford and on to the highway that led to Sydney. We drove past Old Sydney Town and up along the winding roads of the highway. The Sydney to Newcastle expressway was being built at the time. He seemed to be driving more slowly and he kept looking to his left. We rounded a curve and soon after he pulled the car over to the left. I looked around and all I could see was bush on both sides of the road. I quickly got my bearings and thought that perhaps this was where he was going to release me because it was miles from anywhere and he would get away before I could get help. I was ready to get out of the car when he changed gear and reversed the car. I knew then that he had found the spot he had obviously been looking for. Coming off the side of the road on an angle heading back into the bush was a dirt track just wide enough for a car. He reversed back into this, following the track as it curved further back into the bush, leaving the sound of the traffic on the highway behind. I soon lost sight of the road and the realisation hit me that there was no way anyone could see our car. No way anyone could see me.

CHAPTER 3

THE BUSH

In a clearing off the track was the rusted burnt-out shell of a Valiant car. It looked like the skeletal remains of some thief's enjoyment. The man reversed the car into the clearing and parked next to what was left of the Valiant. As he got out of the car, I had my seatbelt off and the passenger door unlocked in a split second but wasn't quick enough. He opened the passenger door, leaned into the car and pulled me up and off the seat. His attitude had changed again and now he was rough and fierce. His hand gripped my right arm tightly and he pulled me across the weeds and short brush grass to the burnt-out wreck and made me stand up against the wreck.

'Stand there and don't do anything stupid,' he growled.

I did as he said, knowing there was nowhere to run. It was a lonely, desolate spot, full of weeds and dirt. He seemed to be familiar with where we were because he was acting confident and was not keeping his voice down or looking around. It was as if he knew there would be no-one coming along to hear us or see us. He wasn't afraid he would be caught and I wondered if he had done this before, perhaps I wasn't the first.

Keeping a tight grip on my arm, he leaned into the back seat of the wreck and pulled at something. With my back against the car, I tried to turn my head but couldn't see what it was. Then he stood up straight and turned to me, releasing his hold on my arm. He moved his head until it was about ten centimetres from my face, brought his right hand up and held his index finger to the end of my nose.

'If you run, you know I'll catch you, don't you?' he threatened.

I couldn't speak. My voice was lost to me, fear was washing over me and drowning me like a tidal wave. I simply nodded my head, my teeth gripping my bottom lip. I stood there, rooted to the spot.

He went back to the back passenger door of the wreck, dragging me with him. I was now standing next to the open door. To stop me running off, he placed his right foot across the front of where I was standing, almost touching the tips of my white sandshoes. He leaned back into the car and he pulled out the bottom section of the back seat. The double seat was once beige-coloured but it was now a dirty brown, frayed and burned. He threw the seat to the ground and told me to get my shirt off.

I stood looking at him, hoping I had misheard what he said. Again he repeated his order, yelling it out this time. I turned away from him and pulled my pink T-shirt over my head. Although I had my swimming costume on underneath, I tried to cover myself up as much as possible. I limply held my shirt across my chest turning back to face him.

He reached towards me and I recoiled from his touch. He laughed, lunged forward and grabbed my shirt. I felt a fierce hatred for him. Still laughing, he turned away and bent down to the seat. He had wanted to use my shirt as a makeshift glove to help him carry the dirty seat. He was now standing in front of me with the seat in his right hand. He took two steps towards me and grabbed my hand, pulling me along after him. He walked towards the dense scrub, which was about two metres tall. He dragged me along a narrow dirt path, moving further into the dense scrub. I was stumbling along behind him. A few metres into the bush was another much smaller clearing.

He stopped and put down the seat. The clearing was hidden by some large rocks—if someone were to walk towards the clearing from that direction, the rocks would have kept us from view. He pushed the seat alongside the rocks, keeping it close to the edge of them so it was partially hidden from view.

'Oh my God, what is going to happen? This is it,' I thought. I tried to keep myself together but my breathing was rapid, my legs felt as if they were going to collapse. He still had hold of my hand and pulled me towards him. Letting go of my hand, he put his hand on my back, pushing me towards the seat, telling me to lie down on it. I froze. I couldn't move and stood there not wanting to hear this, not wanting to be doing this. I just kept standing, staring at him. He loved my humiliation, I could see it on his face. There was a smugness in his voice when he spoke again. He told me to take my clothes off.

Tears sprang to my eyes, my sobs echoing in the surrounding silence. It was early evening and still warm but where I would have expected to hear the sounds of the bush, there was nothing. There was not even the distant hum of the traffic on the highway. It was as if every living creature in the area knew what was going on and was holding its breath along with me, as if they were gripped by the same fear that gripped me. I couldn't understand why this was happening—I was a good girl, I usually did as my parents told me, I wasn't rude to people, I had terrific friends and a wonderful family. Why me?

He stood there looking at me, his arms by his side. The veins at his temple were pulsating steadily and his jaw seemed set in defiance, jutting out towards me. His eyes had narrowed—to me they were like slits of evil. Through his teeth came the order to hurry up.

I was still holding my hands across my chest, trying to cover myself. My arms felt as if they couldn't move but I forced them down by my sides. Hesitatingly, I reached for the waistband of my leggings, bending forward and trying to block out his view of my body. I pulled at the waistband and pulled my leggings down, stepping out of them and holding them in front of me as I straightened up, shielding myself from him. I felt more vulnerable than ever before in my life.

He stared at me, telling me not to stop there or he would take the rest off himself. I couldn't bear the thought of his hands touching me so I slipped down the straps of my costume from my shoulders and pulled my costume off until I stood there naked. I tried to cover my chest with one hand and the lower part of my body with my other hand, slightly bending over to do it. He reached over, placing both his hands on my shoulders and told me: 'You have to give me head again.'

He let one of his hands fall down, grabbed my hand and placed it on the front of his shorts. Holding my hand like a vice, he made me pull down the front of his shorts. He pushed me to my knees on the dirt, forcing me to have oral sex with him. I fought against it and he became impatient. After a minute, he pushed me on to the seat. He was on top of me before I knew what was happening, pinning me down hard. I screamed and yelled out: 'No, no, I don't want to.' I tried to push him away, struggling as much as I could. I forgot all about the pain in my mouth from where he had hit me in the car, forgot about the throbbing in the back of my head where he had punched me with his fist, forgot about the pain in my fingers from scraping them in the boot. I just wanted this to stop, for him to stop.

He pushed down with all his weight and lay on top of me. I couldn't move. He brought his face down until it was only an inch away from mine. He was so close that with each word he spoke, the fringe on my forehead lifted up.

'I don't care if you don't want to, you're just going to have to, darling,' he said. His hand pushed its way between my thighs, forcing them apart as I tried to keep them from parting. His whole upper body was pressed down on me. Then with a quick movement, I felt a burning sensation and the most excruciating pain I have ever felt. It was like being stabbed with a white hot knife. I screamed out in pain, screaming at him not to hurt me anymore but he just looked down at me and laughed. He kept pushing harder and harder, looking at me, listening to me cry and scream. I tried to stop struggling in the hope it would hurt less but it made no difference. He kept himself pressed against me, holding my hands out away from me with his. Then he half lifted himself up with his arms until all his weight was bearing down on his wrists. He looked down on me and asked me to repeat an obscene phrase which he obviously liked—and to call him 'Daddy'. I couldn't believe what he was saying. I couldn't speak. He let go of one of my hands and grabbed at my throat, shouting at me to repeat the phrase. He was getting angry. I said what he had told me to but it wasn't loud enough for him and he told me to say it again. Three times, four times he made me say it, each time telling me to say it louder. When he finished, he sat back on his knees.

I immediately turned on my side on that revolting old car seat, hugging myself and curling up away from him. He grabbed my shoulder closest to him, telling me to turn over. I rolled on to my back again, still with my arms around me and tried to cover myself up. His face seemed to screw up with his anger and the power he must have felt over me. He grabbed me by the hips and threw me over on to my stomach, pulling me up on to my knees.

'Come on, hurry up. You know what I mean. Don't go thinking you can pull this crap,' he said.

So I had to endure the pain of being raped all over again. He told me to say the 'Daddy' phrase again and got very angry because I wouldn't say it loud enough. The rage that had been building up in me finally peaked, I turned around and looking over my right shoulder directly at him screamed out the words he wanted me to say, only I added my own little bit. At the end of the verse, I looked him squarely in the eye and added: 'You bastard.'

I wanted him to see my anger instead of being focused on his own but I came to regret my outburst. He whacked me across the back and then grabbed me by the hips again. Then he started yelling at me, calling me a slut. My anger vanished and was replaced with fear, sheer uncontrollable fear.

He pushed me down on to the seat. I tried to roll away from him as quickly as I could. His legs were blocking mine so I lifted my legs to give me room to move. He was shouting and trying to grab at me. We struggled and I was battering against him with my legs and arms but he managed to pin me down again.

Then the greatest shock hit me. I felt his hands go around my throat and start squeezing. I looked up at him in disbelief. His face was bright red with effort and he was staring down at me. The pressure around my throat increased and I struggled to breathe. My tongue started swelling inside my mouth. 'He's going to kill me, my God, he's going to kill me.' I tried to play dead, holding my breath, letting my body go limp. From what I can now understand, it was at that very moment I lost consciousness. He must have thought he succeeded in his plan and left me alone because the next thing I recall is crawling through the thick, almost impenetrable bush, on my hands and knees, my swimming costume clutched in my hand.

There was a crashing noise behind me and I felt him trying to grab my ankle. He missed a few times as he was having trouble getting through the small gaps in the bush because of his size but I couldn't get away fast enough through the undergrowth, I felt his hand go around my ankle yanking me back towards him. I tried to scream but all I could manage was a hoarse whisper. My throat seared with pain from his attempt to strangle me. I was dragged backwards and over a rock. My head hit the rock and for a moment I thought I would pass out again. Perhaps I did because all I remember is a struggle and waking up, lying face down in the bush with thick leafy branches covering over me. I lay there, pretending I was dead.

My head was pounding and my throat was so sore it felt like there had been a fire down there. Night had fallen. It was pitch black and I couldn't see a thing. For a moment I thought I had been having a nightmare and was really home in bed. In a state of shock, I stood up and walked through the bush with my eyes closed as if I were at home walking from my bedroom into Mum and Dad's room. Once I thought I had made it to their room, I opened my eyes expecting to see them sleeping. Instead it was still dark and I could still smell the bush. It was then that the reality sank in and I fell to my knees, crying as I had never cried before. I screamed for my mum as loud as my throat would allow.

Where was he? Had he gone? Would he come back? Could he see me? Was this part of a game? I think I came as near to reaching breaking point as is possible and I think I would have tipped over the edge had I suddenly not heard a strangely comforting sound, the noise of a truck. The noise snapped me out of my hysteria, bringing me back to the real world. It was a world where Mum would be sick with worry by now. My first thought was of how she would probably have called the police. I had no idea how late it was, only how dark it was. I forced myself to think logically. I could hear the rumble of traffic in the distance coming from behind me and I turned around to face where I thought it came from. I realised I couldn't be far from the highway.

The bush was very dense and I started walking what I thought was straight ahead but after not very long, I lost the sound of the traffic. Then it seemed as if it came from behind me, so I turned around and started in the opposite direction. It was so black, I walked straight into a tree and hit my head hard against the trunk. In complete exhaustion, I fell to my knees, trying to crawl as I felt my way along the ground. The sound of the traffic kept coming from different directions and I became completely confused about where I was supposed to be headed. I was having trouble concentrating. I stood up again and kept moving in a half crouching position so I could feel my way step by step around trees and rocks that I couldn't see but which I knew were there. I became increasingly more desperate each time the sound of the traffic faded into the distance then back within earshot with no idea where it came from. Three times I must have blacked out because three times I woke up to find myself lying on the rocky ground.

I could feel tiny stinging sensations all over my body and felt blood coming from cuts on my legs from the sharp branches I had to push my way through. My throat was so sore it hurt to swallow and I desperately needed water. The pain from my insides was agony and every inch of my body was screaming out. It got so bad, I didn't really know what I was doing, I just felt I had to keep moving because if I stopped, I feared I wouldn't get going again. I would take one step then fall to my knees. Even crawling became difficult and I had to half drag myself along. My whole body was shaking with fear and the cold—I had put my swimming costume back on but the night was bitterly cold here in the hills. My fingers and my feet were numb and I could feel the rest of my body wanting to give in to the cold as well. The traffic seemed almost to be teasing me. Just when I thought I was only a few steps away from the road, it would change direction. Still on my hands and knees, I came up against something hard, a huge boulder. I knew that in this area there were a lot of steep cliffs that dropped away to nothing. I thought this massive rock could be the edge of a cliff. I gingerly reached up and tried to feel across the top of the rock. It reached to a sharp point and then fell away out of my reach. I tried to feel around it but the base of it was too wide for me to measure. The thought of moving along the side of the rock to feel where it went just didn't occur to me. It was like I was programmed, I had to keep going straight ahead. I climbed to the top of the rock and sat there, feeling in front with my feet. I must have sat there for at least thirty minutes, trying to feel my way down the sides of the rock, scared that at any moment I would lose my footing and fall straight down the face of a cliff. With my fingers digging into the rock, I lowered myself inch by inch down the face of it before my feet finally touched solid ground. The rock turned out to be no more than that—a rock. It was about one and a half metres wide and maybe a metre high.

My sense of hopelessness overwhelmed me and all I could do was huddle up and cry. The ordeal drained any energy I had left. I was freezing, tired, scared and alone. I lay among some thick tall grass, grabbing as much of it as I could and pulled it over me. I drew my knees up to my chest and used the grass to try to keep myself warm. I lay there for what seemed an eternity trying to gather some strength.

There was a rustling sound in the bush behind me. I froze, holding my breath. My God, I thought, what if it's him again? What if he has been following me this whole time? I tried to calm myself down, knowing that if he had been behind me, he would have had plenty of opportunity to attack me again. I lay there as still as possible. Hearing the sound again, I realised it was an animal of some kind. It was a scurrying sound, not loud enough to have been made by a human. I felt movement behind my back and then felt a warm, small furry body with sharp claws scramble up my back, across my hips and down near my stomach. I was lying on my side and my new companion curled up against my stomach for about ten minutes. It was a noisy little thing but I was so thankful for the contact with something that didn't hurt me that I enjoyed the sounds it made. Then it left, leaving me alone again. I'm almost certain it was a possum because as it left I could feel its tail brush against my leg and I was able to make out the little curl at the end of it.

I remained huddled up, trying to cover myself as much as possible. I thought my only chance was to wait for the sun to rise. Walking in the dark was taking too much out of me and I needed to wait until I could see where I was going. I managed to fall asleep and when I awoke, I was relieved to see the sun rising on the horizon. I could see the tree tops and make out the shapes in the bush. I was shocked when I looked around me and saw what I had been walking through. The bush was so thick that I had been walking through what looked like a solid mass of tangled tree and bush roots. There had only been a gap about a metre high off the ground through which I had crawled.

I could see dried blood covered my legs which were scratched all over from the bush. My left foot was throbbing, looking down I saw a huge gash embedded with grass and twigs. I cleaned out what I could from my foot and tried to stand. As I straightened up, a wave of nausea came over me. I steadied myself by leaning up against a tree and took a few deep breaths. Using the tree for support, I listened intently until I could hear the traffic again. All through the night, I had only had the idea of flagging down a truck, not a car. The thought of getting in another car was so frightening to me that I could not do it. I moved towards the sound of the traffic and it seemed less arduous than it had during the night because at least I could see where I was going. This time, when the sound of the traffic changed direction, I kept heading in the original direction I had chosen. I came to a massive dense bush that panned out at least three and a half metres. It was like a wall and completely blocked any view of the other side. I walked along the side of it until I found a small spot where I could climb over. As I swung my legs across the rim of the bush, I saw a flash of light and heard the sound of traffic again.

I stood on the other side of the bush watching for another flash of light. It was then, and only then, that my spirits lifted and I thought I might finally reach safety. I saw another flash of light and then another. I realised the flashes were the early morning sun reflecting off the cars driving past. I tried to run towards the area the flashes came from but the pain that surged through my body stopped me in my tracks. I shuffled the rest of the way. All my concentration was focused purely on getting closer to the road. When I was within a few metres of it, I saw huge boulders just to my left by the side of the road. I moved back into the bush and made my way over to the boulders, using them as cover to hide behind. What I was afraid of more than anything was that the man might still be in the area watching and waiting to see if I had managed to get to the road.

I hid as a car went by and sank back further behind the cover of the boulders as more cars passed. The road went down a slight hill and I was able to see the traffic coming up the hill towards me. I guessed it was about six o'clock as there still weren't many cars on the road. I had to wait some time between each car or groups of cars. I had been behind the boulders for about half an hour when I heard a truck. There it was rounding the bend and heading in my direction. I waited for it to get closer to me, then I stepped out from my hiding place on to the right-hand shoulder of the road and started to wave frantically. The truck was only metres away. I stepped back in the bush in case a car was coming from the opposite direction, in case the man was coming back and would see me there. Then I panicked about the truck missing me. A loud hissing sound filled the air and I realised it was the air brakes of the truck. It came to a stop with a screech of tyres.

CHAPTER 4

THE POLICE

I raced across the road to the truck which had come to a stop a fair way down the road and ran along the left-hand side towards the passenger door. I was so focused on getting into that truck and reaching safety that I didn't even think about the driver and what he would make of all this. I was frozen to the bone but my adrenalin was pumping. Beneath the passenger door were small ladder-like steps which I scrambled up to reach the door handle. I was shaking so much that I nearly fell off them as I tried to support my weight with my right arm while reaching up to open the door with my left hand.

I pulled myself up into the passenger seat and looked across to the driver's side. It was empty! In my rush to get off the road, into the truck and out of sight I had failed to notice that there were two trucks travelling in convoy. It had been the first truck that I had flagged down and here I was in the second truck. I wasn't sure what to do and was about to climb back out on to the road when outside the driver's side window appeared two men. One of them had a puzzled look on his face and was looking up and down the road. I could hear him telling his mate: 'There was a girl standing over there on the side of the road flagging me down.'

As the two men looked around, I leaned forward in the cabin of the truck and banged frantically on the windscreen. They both looked up and to say they were surprised to see me sitting there was an understatement. The taller of them walked straight up to the driver's door and climbed into his seat. He looked across at me, huddled in the corner of the cab wearing just my swimming costume and shook his head in disbelief. In a quiet voice he said: 'Oh God, what's happened to you?'

I lost what control I had and started shivering violently.

'A man took me into the bush,' I stuttered.

'Oh, Jesus,' he said and he reached behind his seat and pulled out a blanket from the cabin. He leaned over to wrap the blanket around me but pulled back and first asked in an urgent voice,

'Are you hurt?'

He was looking with concern at my lower ribcage area. I looked down and saw a large apple-sized blood stain on the right-hand side of my torso.

'I don't think so,' I said. 'Please help me.'

It was all I could do to look at him. I couldn't say any more.

'Don't you worry, honey, no-one can hurt you now. My name's John. We'll get you out of here, OK.'

He reached down beside his seat and pulled up a thermos flask. Unscrewing the lid, he poured some coffee into it and handed it to me, saying, 'This should warm you up.'

I took it gratefully but when I tried to sip the hot coffee, it hurt my throat. My throat and neck were so badly swollen that I couldn't swallow without flinching. John saw me bringing my hand up to my throat and tears starting to run down my cheeks. Shaking his head, he muttered, 'What did that bastard do to you?'

It was more of a statement than a question and I just looked at him.

John started up the engine and I saw that the truck that had been parked in front of us was still there. A crackle sounded in the cabin and John picked up the small black handset of his CB radio and held it in front of his mouth, waiting to hear who wanted him.

'John, what the hell is going on? What was she doing out there?' It was the driver of the first truck.

'Some bastard attacked her,' John replied and left it at that.

He pressed his fingers down again on the button on the handset and asked if there was anyone listening who could give him directions to the nearest police station. Someone came back with the route to the station in Gosford.

The journey to Gosford was a bit of a blur for me as we sped along the highway. A few times drivers called up John over the CB radio asking about what had happened. He simply told them to shut up, saying, 'Stop talking about it. I think she's been through enough. She doesn't need to hear you lot go on about it.'

A few drivers called through and said sorry. Then John turned down the volume to make sure I heard no more of the discussion. The radio fell silent.

We reached the outskirts of town and when I saw I was in an area I was able to recognise, I started to feel more secure. I was marvelling at the speed at which the semi-trailer was being driven. John had a full load of logs he had been moving north from Sydney but despite the heavy load, we were driving so fast that the wheels were screaming around corners. There wasn't much more conversation between the two of us. I think John was in almost as much shock as I was.

John ran all the red lights on Gosford main street, sounding his loud air horns all the way. We pulled up in front of the police station with another squeal of tyres.

'Stay there, I'll come around and get you,' John ordered.

He swung down from the cab and soon had my door open. As he held out his hand to help me out, he looked down at the floor of the cabin and asked me if I felt any pain. I was confused and looked down at my feet, wondering what he was talking about. To my surprise, there was another blood stain, this time the size of a small pizza pan. The stain had been made by the gash in my foot that was now bleeding because of my movement through the bush. John looked at me and all I could do was shake my head, shrug my shoulders and say I was sorry. He smiled and told me not to worry about it. He then reached in, scooped me up in his arms and carried me into the police station. With me draped in the blanket, John pushed through the station's doors and carried me into the foyer, calling out,

'Can somebody help us here?'

I looked around, hardly able to believe I was safe. It had an almost surreal feel to it. To the right-hand side of the entrance was a long open counter with the desk sergeant, a grey-haired officer in uniform, standing behind it. His head snapped up and he looked us over. Then he asked for my name. When I told him who I was, the action kicked in.

'Just the little lady we've been looking for,' he said.

The desk sergeant then looked at John and asked,

'And who are you?'

Still cradling me in his arms, John told him in a few brief words what had happened. As the desk sergeant walked around from behind the counter, he directed John to take me into a room that was behind us, to the left side of the main doors. We went through to what looked like a conference room, empty except for a blackboard on the far wall and a table with two chairs set against the right-hand wall. John carried me over to the table and placed me gently down into one of the chairs facing the door. He pulled the other chair across and sat down next to me, putting an arm around my shoulders.

'It'll be all right now, honey,' he said.

The desk sergeant came into the room and asked John to follow him. John turned to me with a look that asked if I would be all right. The sergeant asked again for John to go with him. I held on to John's hand, not wanting him to leave me. I felt comfortable for the first time in what seemed like ages and I didn't want him to go. It was as if he had become my security blanket. I knew he had to go because I realised the sergeant had some questions for him. I told John how grateful I was and thanked him for all the help he had given me. He simply laid a hand on my shoulder and nodded his head before he left.

As he walked out of the room with the sergeant, a female officer walked in. She came over to me and introduced herself as Sue. I later learned she was Susan Gray. She told me my mum and dad had been called and were on their way in. Sue asked if I was in any pain and I shook my head. I could feel myself shrinking down into the chair, shivering. Sue looked around the room and asked if I would be OK if she left me alone for a minute. Almost immediately she was back with a leather police jacket under her arm.

'Here you go, sweetheart. Pop this around your shoulders, you must be freezing,' she said. She also brought in a mug of coffee and although I couldn't drink it, I was grateful for it because it warmed my hands to hold it. Sue and I spoke for a few minutes although she didn't ask me for any details about what had happened. She was more concerned about my injuries. She had noticed the blood on my swimming costume and the blood which had now spread on the carpet from my foot. She brought some bandages and tried her best to bandage my foot and make sure I was warm enough. I was trying not to be a nuisance.

We both looked up as the door opened and a man of medium height, strong build with dark hair, a round face and very kind eyes walked in. He introduced himself as Detective Senior Constable Brian Collis. Sue excused herself and the detective and I looked at each other. He still remembers that moment vividly: 'I remember the blonde hair and this little girl, cut to pieces.'

Brian asked how I was doing and moved straight on to ask about John— How had I come into contact with him, where had I first seen him? John must have been their initial suspect although they soon realised he was not only innocent but my saviour. Another officer came into the room and Brian introduced him as Detective Senior Constable Rick Ashton. They were very concerned about me. After a short time, Brian left the room and returned to tell me Mum and Dad were here.

I really had no idea what to expect from them. The enormity of what had happened the previous night hadn't really hit me. I was sort of expecting Dad to be really angry at me for getting in that car. I knew I had done the wrong thing.

Again the door opened and this time Mum burst in. I had never seen her looking so anxious. She was almost running as she crossed the floor towards me. She bent down to the chair and hugged me, telling me everything would be all right and that she loved me very much. As her arms went around me, I was overcome with pure relief. Nothing will ever replace the feeling of being held by Mum at that time. It was all I had longed for all through that long, cold, awful night. Dad had been standing a short distance behind Mum and he came up to me, ruffled my hair and said: 'How are you going, kid?' ('Kid' was Dad's pet name for me.)

Mum was trying hard to keep it together but I could see the tears forming in her eyes. Poor Mum, she had just been through the worst night of her life. It was just a few hours ago that she had been looking forward to the three of us spending a nice quiet evening together. After I had left, Mum had gone to the hairdresser in the morning, had a new haircut and was feeling really good. It was a luxury for her to have time to herself and she pottered about in the flat in the afternoon making me my favourite dinner, tuna casserole. She was on holiday, she was relaxed and happy.

As it got close to 4.30 p.m., Mum waited out on the balcony where she had a view of the main street. But the bus came and went and after waiting for fifteen minutes, she started wondering where I could be. By five o'clock she was getting a little concerned. Being September, the days were warm but the evening had already started to get chilly. By 5.30 p.m. she knew there was something wrong because I was never late without letting her know. She knew that if I stayed with friends, I always rang her—always. She waited until 5.45 p.m. and by then she knew that something was very wrong. But Dad still wasn't home and Mum didn't know what to do.

She walked up to The Entrance Police Station a block away and spoke to a young constable on the desk, telling him how she was really worried about her daughter because I had been due home at 4.30 p.m. and it was now 5.45 p.m. and dark outside. She became even more upset because the officer appeared totally disinterested, telling her to wait a bit longer. Back at the flat, she started frantically ringing my girlfriends, starting with Susie and Cathy. They told her how they had last seen me when I left the beach at about 3.30 p.m. heading home. It made Mum even more worried. She ran back up to the police station and once again they were very cold with her. She felt they treated her like a neurotic mother behaving in a silly manner. She begged them to please, please do something but the young constable told her to give it a few more hours. He said I was probably just staying overnight with friends. He did say they would keep an eye out for me and Mum gave them a description of what I looked like and what I was wearing. She walked back to the flat feeling very, very alone. All she could do was make more phone calls to more of my friends, none of whom had any good news for her.

When she saw Dad's car pull up, she ran downstairs and told him what had happened. She had decided she needed to speak to Susie face to face because she figured that if I was out with friends and Susie was covering up for me, she wanted Susie to know that nothing else mattered but finding me. No-one would be in trouble if she just told the truth.

By the time they got to Susie's front door, it was 6.30 p.m. and Mum was frantic. Susie told Mum she was telling the truth about the last time she had seen me, I had definitely been heading for the bus stop on my way home. Mum already feared something was wrong but speaking directly to Susie confirmed it for her.

Mum and Dad raced back home just in case I had turned up. The flat suddenly seemed very empty and more silent than ever before. Mum walked into my room but it was still the way she had left it half an hour earlier. The tuna casserole was still in the oven and the smell filled the flat. Once again Mum rang the local police and once again, they asked for a description. The police told her that if the patrol cars spotted me, they would get in touch but Mum still felt they were placating her and had no real intention of looking for me.

Unable to sit still, Mum and Dad got back in the car and drove around the streets. It was a desperate idea but they thought they might just spot me. For a couple of hours, they drove around the area, regularly returning home hoping to find me there waiting for them. Mum began to worry I would get home and find no-one there so she decided to stay at the flat while Dad continued to search the streets by car. It was the worst thing she could have done because she felt useless, just pacing up and down, her arms hugged around her body, shaking, constantly walking out on to that balcony off the lounge room and looking into the darkness. It was freezing outside and even in the flat she felt so cold she kept her coat on inside. She stood on the balcony for ages, looking out into the night, praying, really praying for the first time in her life. Praying I was OK and was just pulling some silly stunt and I'd be home soon with a silly excuse. Deep down she knew, she knew I was in trouble.

She rang her sister who lived in Queensland and told her what had happened. My Aunt Billie, to whom I am very close, shared Mum's fears. This wasn't like me; I always rang if I was going to be late. When Dad got back, Mum joined him in the car and they drove around again. They didn't know what they were looking for or where to look, they just knew they had to do something. At one point, a police car with lights flashing pulled them over. Mum threw the door open and was out of the car before it even stopped in case they had some news of me. However they had stopped Dad because a brake light was out. Mum yelled and screamed at the officer, telling him that he should be out looking for her daughter instead of picking people up because of faulty brake lights. The officer said nothing and drove off in silence.

When they got home and still I wasn't there, Mum began praying that I wasn't dead. By this time, it was about 11.30 p.m. and she even rang radio and television stations and newspapers asking if they had heard any news of a missing girl. She rang hospitals to see if I had been in an accident. Between these calls, she was ringing the police every few minutes, asking them to put out bulletins of what I was wearing, what I looked like. While ringing all these people, she was worried I would be trying to get through to her on the phone, so she couldn't hang up quickly enough. She sat by the radio and had the TV switched on at the same time hoping she would hear something about me.

Dad fell asleep on the couch while Mum was frantic not knowing where her little girl was, just knowing I was out there all alone. She kept pacing and crying, trying to will me to her. She was praying: 'Please God, please, please, please God, please God help her.' She kept walking out on the balcony, feeling closer to me there because it was the last place she had seen me. She hoped against hope that I would come walking out of the darkness saying: 'Hi, Mum, sorry I'm late.'

Even though Mum was up all night, the hours passed quite quickly. At about two in the morning she broke down, weeping, feeling totally lost and helpless. Dad was still asleep and Mum felt all alone, not knowing what to do. She was clutching at anything, any shred. She went through my drawers looking for letters or notes or some clue as to where I might have gone. Had I been upset? Had there been something worrying me? Had I run away? She was totally exhausted but her mind wouldn't stop. She went on hoping and praying, hoping and pacing, praying and looking out into the dark.

At four o'clock she rang my Aunt Billie again and the first thing my aunt asked was had I been found yet. Then she said she was flying straight down to be with Mum. She booked herself on the first flight to Sydney, rang her boss, waking him up to say she wouldn't be in at work and by five o'clock that morning was at the airport waiting for the plane to leave.

At about seven o'clock the phone rang and Mum flew across the room. It was Gosford police. For those first few seconds everything stood still. The policeman said: 'We've found your daughter.' He said I was OK and would Mum and Dad be able to get to the police station.

The relief was overwhelming.

Speaking nineteen to the dozen, Mum woke Dad and told him I was OK, I was at the police station, they had to go, they had to get there quickly. She doesn't remember the drive to the police station. As soon as Dad pulled up on the opposite side of the road, Mum was out and dashing across the road, not even looking for traffic. She ran into the police station, Dad finally caught up with her.

'Where's my daughter? Where's my daughter?' she asked the desk sergeant.

She thought she must have looked a fright. She hadn't slept, her hair was all over the place and she was still wearing the coat she had not taken off all night. She had a wild look in her eyes. The desk sergeant told her they wanted to talk to her for a few minutes before she saw me. Mum thought they would tell her they found me in Sydney and had brought me back. By this time she thought I'd done something silly like running away or having an adventure in town with a friend. She didn't expect what she was about to be told. The desk sergeant led Mum and Dad to a little interviewing room where they saw Sue, the policewoman.

'I just want to see my daughter, please. Is she here? Could we do this later?' Mum was pleading with her.

Sue asked them to sit down. She looked at Mum and said: 'Oksanna, we need you to be strong and your daughter needs you to be strong.'

Mum looked back at her and, still with no inkling of what was coming, said: 'Well, OK, I'm strong.'

Sue said I was at the police station and I was alive.

'Well, when can I see her?' said Mum.

'Oksanna, she's been raped.'

It didn't register with Mum. She just looked at Sue and Sue repeated those four words. They sat for a few seconds in silence. Then Mum said: 'OK, can I see her now?' It was more important to her that I was alive.

Sue said: 'We'll take you in to see her now. She's a bit of a mess but she's OK and you have to be strong for her. Please don't break down when you see her. It's very important that she sees your reaction as being strong.'

When Mum saw me in the conference room, I could tell she was trying hard to do just that, to be strong and not let me see how upset and worried she was. As she hugged me, I kept saying to her: 'I'm OK, Mum, I'm OK, please don't worry.'

I noticed she kept looking me up and down, something everyone was doing but I couldn't understand why. Brian Collis came back into the room and engaged in a discussion with Mum and Dad. I heard Mum ask about taking me home but Brian said I would have to go to the hospital first for an examination.

While everyone's attention was elsewhere and I wasn't being watched, I pulled the blanket away from myself to look at what had transfixed them all. For the first time I looked at my feet and legs and saw they resembled road maps splattered with blood. My swimming costume was ripped and had marks all over it. My arms were badly scratched and bloody from my shoulders down to my hands and fingers. I ran one hand over my face and could feel all the scratches and clotted blood. No wonder everyone had been looking at me so intently. Suddenly I longed for a hot shower and clean clothes to cover the wounds.

Brian had finished talking to Mum and Dad. He turned to me and explained that I had to be taken up to the hospital. He asked if that was all right. I was feeling so numb that I just nodded my head. Mum asked Dad if he would go home and pick me up some clean, warm clothes and meet us there. Brian introduced another officer to us, Michael Upton, and explained he would also be working on my case. A second policewoman, a slim woman with short dark hair called Kerrie McDonald, also joined us. They led Mum and me out of the room, through the rear of the building to a car park where we got into the back of an unmarked police car. On the way to the hospital, Brian told us the hospital was expecting us. I wasn't really paying too much attention. My mind seemed not to want to focus on too much. I felt like I should have been screaming and crying but I felt removed from what was happening around me. It was as if it was happening to someone else and I was just an onlooker. Even the fact that there were all these police around me, taking care of me, didn't faze me.

At the hospital, I was taken through the Accident and Emergency entrance. The woman sitting behind the counter looked up as we entered. Rick Ashton simply said 'Gosford Police' and the woman nodded her head.

She stood up and led us into a small waiting room explaining someone would see us shortly. She returned with some forms for us to fill in. Mum was doing her best to help and tried to fill them in as quickly as possible. She had hardly let me go since we were reunited at the police station and she was sitting with her arms around me when the nurse walked in.

The nurse said they had called in a female doctor especially for me and she would be with me soon. She explained how the doctor needed to take samples from me, including scrapings from under my nails, and needed to conduct an internal examination. I just looked at Mum. The last thing I wanted was anyone touching me, let alone an internal examination. I could see Mum felt the same way and tears sprang to her eyes. I felt so sorry for putting Mum through this, knowing in a way it was my own fault. I was the one who put myself in that stranger's car.

The doctor arrived and introduced herself as Dr Shearer. Mum asked me: 'Do you want me to go in with you, darling?' She was concerned that I wanted privacy but I wanted Mum to be there with me. I had never been in a hospital before and had no idea what to expect. The room we were taken into was quite small. It had a trolley-style bed along the left-hand wall. Along the right-hand wall was a tall metal table with lots of metal instruments on the top. I noticed how the bright hospital lights reflected off them. A nurse joined us in the room and she had such a kind face that she made me feel relaxed with her. Kerrie McDonald was also there. I later learned she had to be the witness to the examination so all the evidence could be handed over to the police forensic people.

Dr Shearer asked me not to sit down but to stand as still as possible. She turned to the table and pulled out some large sheets of paper from under a tray and placed them on the floor. She asked me to stand on the paper and to remove my swimsuit as carefully as I could. She explained that by doing it this way, anything that came off with the swimsuit would fall on the paper and could be used as evidence if needed. As I took it off, the nurse held up a hospital gown and helped me into it. I stood to one side and the nurse pulled on some plastic gloves, picked up my swimsuit and put it into a bag.

Then she picked up the sterile paper and that also went into another bag. I was then asked to stand on another piece of paper while the nurse ran an instrument that looked like a large wooden spoon along the base of each foot. This sheet of paper was also folded up and placed into a bag. The doctor then asked me to sit on the bed. I hadn't noticed up to that point but she had been talking into a small cassette recorder while I had been undressing. She asked me to tell her what had happened. This was the first time I had to really speak about the attack. It was difficult for me and I didn't know if I could do it. Then I thought that if I didn't, the man could possibly do this to someone else. I didn't go into too much detail, just told the doctor the basics, that I had been raped several times and that the man tried to choke me. I became acutely aware of Mum and I felt an overwhelming guilt. I could see how hard this was for her but Mum was still being so strong for me and that helped me to get through it.

As I told the doctor about each injury she would tend to that area. When I told her about being hit across the face in the car, she asked me to open my mouth and looked inside. She told her tape recorder that there were bruising and teeth marks inside my cheeks. She felt around my neck and noted there was bruising there that resembled two hand marks. She said she had to do the internal examination and started to pull the curtain around the bed. I looked across at Mum, knowing the curtain would block out her being able to see me. Mum looked at me and I could tell she had been sitting there quietly crying.

'Do you want me to stay, darling?' she asked.

I asked her to stay with me and Mum reached out and grabbed my hand, saying: 'I'll be right here.'

Dr Shearer did an internal examination. She noted inflammation and torn skin and took samples and swabs. She had to use a special instrument to do this which made me wince in pain. The nurse came over to me and held my other hand. The pain wasn't bad enough to warrant tears but I couldn't control myself, silent tears flowed down my cheeks. For the first time that day I really cried. The nurse stood there looking down at me and her grip on my hand tightened. I noticed she also had tears in her eyes.

'Hang in there, pet, it'll be over soon,' she said.

The examination over, the nurse put a blanket around me and passed me a glass of orange juice and some sandwiches with the crusts cut off. Dr Shearer said I would probably have trouble swallowing for a while but that I should try to eat and drink something to regain my strength.

The nurse got some towels and said she'd show me where the showers were and said she would sit right outside the shower in case I needed her. Mum asked if there was anything she could do for me but I told her I was OK. We held each other close again and Mum said she'd go to the toilet while I had a shower. Unknown to me at the time, as soon as she got to the toilet Mum grabbed a thick fistful of paper hand towels, pushed them into her mouth and screamed and screamed into them until her throat was sore. She cried, sobbing loudly, and then looked at herself in the mirror. 'She's alive, she's alive, she's alive. I have to be strong,' she said to herself.

In the shower, I was looking forward to the soothing feel of warm water running over me but the instant I stepped under the water, the pain that washed over me made me jump back out against the tiled wall. I hadn't thought about the scratches and open wounds that covered my body. The pain was like when you cut yourself shaving, the instant the water gets into the cut it stings. Because I had cuts all over, the stinging was so bad it left me shivering. Little by little I stepped under the shower, gritting my teeth each time the water reached a new area of skin. It took me at least five minutes to get under the shower fully. The pain eventually subsided and the warm water flowing over my skin was heavenly.

I had been given some soap and it was wonderful to smell the cleanness of the soap instead of the smell of the bush which had lingered on me. I lathered the soap and started to wash myself carefully but the gentle soothing action soon turned into a fierce scrubbing. I just wanted to be clean. I scrubbed and scrubbed. Under my nails, my feet, my face, my hair. My skin started hurting but I didn't care—I just wanted to be rid of anything that may still have been on me. I finally decided it was time to get out when the nurse stuck her head around the door and asked if I was all right. After my hot shower and feeling snug in the warm clothes Dad had brought back for me, I started to feel very tired. Mum and I sat down next to each other and I just fell into her as she put her arms around me, cradled me. Mum wanted to take me home to rest but the police had other ideas. They wanted me to go back to the station and make a statement. Mum was horrified and pleaded with them, saying she felt I had had enough and I wasn't up to it. Brian Collis said it was important that I give them as much information as possible now, while it was still fresh in my mind. I took Mum's hand and said: 'It's all right, Mum, I want to get this over.' Mum could see I was certain about it and she just nodded her head.

'OK, honey, as long as you're sure. You don't have to yet if you don't want to,' she said. I knew the police were right and that I should talk about the attack as soon as I could. I wanted to do everything I could to get the man who did this.

'I know, Mum, but I'm OK,' I said.

Back at Gosford Police Station, Kerrie McDonald joined Mum and me in a small room filled with a huge table. As I went through the previous night word by word, action by action, Kerrie typed it all out. I remembered the interior of his car, what he had been wearing, the cane cigarette lighter and matching cigarette case, the contents of the shelf beneath the glovebox, the contents of the boot. I told Kerrie about the fingerprints I'd left in the boot and the false fingernails I'd hidden behind the brake lights. I could only remember a couple of letters of his licence plate number.

When I got to the part about the sexual assault, I heard myself lowering my voice. I didn't want Mum to hear this. I needn't have worried because Mum had tuned out by this time. She was numb and didn't hear a thing about the attack. She didn't want to. When we finished, Kerrie handed me the statement and I read and signed each page. Reading through it seemed to make what had happened all the more real to me.

All that talking had made my throat hurt even more. Mum brought me a glass of water and as I was sipping it, waiting to go home, Rick Ashton came in and said the forensic photographer had arrived. He explained they now needed to take some photos of my injuries.

The photographer was waiting for Mum and me in another room. He introduced himself and tried to put me at ease but when I was asked to remove my clothes, leaving only my underwear on, I stopped and took a breath for a minute. Mum was right there by my side and I clung to her. I didn't want anyone else to look at me. I wanted to go home. I knew the police had to do their job. 'OK, let's do this,' I said.

When I had taken off my clothes, the photographer positioned me against a large sheet of white paper which hung on the wall behind me. He took photos of my neck and face and all my limbs to show the cuts and the bruises which were now starting to show. It was a very cold and clinical business and I felt like I was being ordered around by a drill sergeant. Thankfully, it didn't take very long.

Meanwhile the detectives had my statement and, using a huge map pinned on the wall, had been trying to trace the route the man and I had travelled along. The detectives explained to me that they needed to pinpoint the exact locations of each incident. They asked if I could help them and it was as if I kicked into remote control, as if I was seeing this in the third person. I pointed out to them where I believed we had made turns, and what happened at each point. Then Michael Upton asked for one more thing— would I be prepared to go out with the police and lead them to the last spot I had been taken? That clearing in the bush. The rape scene. I looked at Mum and for the first time she cried openly in front of me.

'I'd prefer it if you didn't go,' she said.

I felt so sorry for her. She had tried to be strong but she couldn't bring herself to come with me. We hugged tightly and I left her at the police station while I went off with the detectives.

Two police cars headed out to Wamberal and started at the point where I had been picked up. I was very clear on the route, directing Brian confidently. When we got to the area where the man first forced me to have oral sex, I got a bit confused about which way we went. It took me a while to find the driveway with the letterboxes but as soon as I found the spot, I knew that was the right place.

Then we headed out to Kariong to the old highway that overlooked the construction of what was to be the F3 freeway between Sydney and Newcastle. We drove along the same stretch a few times trying to find the dirt side road. It was hard to see because it curved back at an angle. I was able to show the police the spot where I came on to the road and flagged down the trucks. It was just as we headed back along the road for another search that I spotted the dirt track. Michael pointed out there was no way anyone would have been able to find it if they hadn't known it was there. We drove through the bush into the clearing. There, just as I had described, the police saw the burnt-out wreck of the car. We all got out of the cars and as the photographer took pictures, I stood there and looked. It had felt desolate the night before, now in the light of day it still felt spooky. I felt as though I was watching all this in a movie, a horror movie.

Brian walked over and asked where the second clearing was, the one where the car seat would be. I pointed in the direction. Turning to Kerrie, I asked if I could stay in the car and she said she'd stay right there with me, but when I heard Rick Ashton call out they had found the spot, for some reason I felt I had to go and take a look for myself. I asked Kerrie to come with me and we headed along the narrow dirt track through the gum trees and tall prickly scrub to where the others stood.

There it was, that horrible filthy car seat on the ground. When I saw it, I fell apart and started to cry. My shoes and white tights were still lying on the ground and it was obvious there had been a struggle. Kerrie put her arm around me and led me away. We stood by the cars as I calmed down. When the others returned, one of them was carrying the seat, which would have to be tested and used as possible evidence. The police were very understanding. Michael and Brian came straight over, Michael putting his arm around me and asking if I was all right.

● ● ●

Back at the station, the only thing left for me to do that day was have my fingerprints taken so if they found the car they could match them to the prints in the boot. Finally, Mum, Dad and I were in the car, on our way home. The trip was made in silence. We were all completely exhausted and in shock. We just shared a sense of relief that I was back with them.

At the flat, Aunt Billie was there waiting with the door open. She started crying as we hugged tightly. Then Mum and her sister fell into each other's arms. It was strange walking back into the flat, my home. I felt as if I had been away for years. Everything looked familiar but I seemed to be looking at it from a distance. It was still only about lunchtime and my aunt had made lunch, saying it was ready to be reheated whenever we were ready to eat but all I wanted to do was to climb into my bed. I was dead on my feet. It felt so good to crawl between the sheets, to finally be in bed after wishing for it during the night in the bush. Mum sat on the bed, holding me and stroking my hair the way she used to when I was little. I felt myself dozing off in a lovely warm cocoon. Suddenly I was awake. I'd had a flashback to the night before. I got up and walked out to the lounge room, thinking I must have slept for ages but Mum said I'd only been in bed about thirty minutes.

The rest of that afternoon and evening passed slowly and strangely. The three of us, Mum, my aunt and myself, usually never stop talking, we are quite notorious for it in our family but that day there wasn't much said at all between us. Mum and I followed each other around. Every time I moved into another room, she went with me and I did the same with her. I felt safe near her. I tried a couple of times to sleep but each time woke up with nightmares almost as soon as I shut my eyes. Unknown to me, as I napped Mum slipped into her bedroom and cried into her pillow, then wiped her eyes and came out again trying to be strong for me. I think everyone was trying to anticipate my emotions. If I wanted to talk, then they did too, but if I wanted to sit quietly, they wouldn't speak either.

As the evening wore on, I started to ache all over and found it hard to sit in one position for any length of time. Mum was fussing around but one look at her and I could see how exhausted she was, so I finally said I was going to bed. Mum lay down with me and this time I fell straight to sleep.

Through the night I woke up screaming again and Mum grabbed me. I cried and cried into her arms and she rocked me back and forth, telling me it was all right, that she was there and she would never let anyone hurt me again. We went into the lounge because I knew I wouldn't get back to sleep straight away. We sat down, Mum with a coffee, me with warm milk and honey that Mum had made to try to soothe my throat. Dad came out and had a cigarette. When he went back to bed, Mum and I just sat there in the darkness watching TV. We still didn't speak about what had happened. I wasn't ready and I knew Mum would wait so there was no pressure on me.

I went back to bed but I woke up numerous times. Luckily I didn't wake anyone up and for the first time, I was able to grab some time on my own. Awake or asleep, the attack kept flooding through my mind. I kept thinking back to those times when I had a chance to run, to try to get away and hated myself for not doing so. I felt almost as if I had deserved what had happened. I didn't want to see anyone again because I felt so ashamed.

When dawn came on Thursday, I was already awake and feeling more tired than before I had gone to bed. Mum was soon up and so was my aunt. We tried to have some breakfast but we didn't have much luck, none of us had much of an appetite. The police rang about 9.30 and said they were sending around a car for us. Mum and I were showered, dressed and waiting when the car got there half an hour later to take us back to the police station. The detectives had been up most of the night and Brian and Rick were waiting for us. I was starting to feel comfortable with them, I felt as if they cared about how I was handling everything. This time they needed me to do an Identikit picture of the stranger with the help of a police artist. I had thought the artist would have had a book containing different sections with eyes, noses and mouths and that I could just pick from them to form a face that resembled the man. All he had in front of him were a few pencils and a sketchpad.

Mum and I sat for about one-and-a-half-hours with the artist before Mum asked if I could have a break. I had been trying my best to explain the features but each time he tried to draw what I had explained, it looked wrong. He was experienced at this sort of thing and very patient, but I wasn't. Trying to remember the exact shape of the man's eyes, his mouth, his nose, was not as easy as I thought it would have been. I was getting so frustrated with myself because I felt I was taking up the time of the police. I felt as if I was letting everyone down.

The detectives were great. They told me not to be hard on myself and to take as long as I wanted to get the Identikit right. After a short break, I was able to describe my attacker a little better and we soon had the sketch finished. When it was done, I wasn't ready for it. Seeing all the individual features brought together, I found myself looking into the eyes of the man who attacked me and it was very difficult. I felt scared all over again.

As it turned out, the sketch was an almost perfect match. I was told it became one of those used for training purposes at the New South Wales Police scientific section in Sydney, kept in a book with the sketch on one side and a photograph of the man on the other. Brian cracked a few jokes to try to relax me. I felt we were all becoming friends. Michael said he was the father of one of the girls I knew at school, we were in the same year. He passed on her best wishes. It felt strange to hear about someone from school, it seemed so removed from where I was now. Gosford Police Station was all that I knew at that moment and I felt so entrenched there that I felt I couldn't reach out to that other part of my life. School, friends, everything seemed so distant. I wanted to be back there so much.

CHAPTER 5

THE ARREST

It was the confidence of the police that kept me going. 'Give us a couple of days and we'll catch the man who did this to you,' said Brian Collis, making it sound almost like a promise, as he and Rick Ashton drove Mum and me home. I said I couldn't believe they would be able to find him so quickly but Brian made a joke out of it saying there would be no problem because they were such top detectives. If he was trying to give me a boost and put me at ease, it worked.

Back at the flat, my best friend Alison was waiting for me. Word had got around very quickly about what had happened as it does in small communities, and Aunt Billie had been fielding telephone calls and turning away visitors all morning while Mum and I were at the police station. Aunt Billie knew of the close bond Ali and I shared so she had invited her to stay and wait. Ali and I have always been able to relate well so it was a great relief to find her waiting for me with her smiling friendly face. She had been sitting on the lounge and stood up as we walked through the door. She came over to us and put her arms around Mum and me before any of us said a word.

'Look, I'm not here to get all the details or hear all the gore. I'm here if you need someone to talk to. If you don't want to talk about it, that's fine with me but just know I'm here for you guys,' she said. The three of us and my aunt all started crying. Seeing Ali gave me the sense of reality I needed. For a short time it made me feel that what had happened wasn't as bad as I thought because my old life was still there. At that moment she was exactly what the doctor would have ordered for me.

The kettle was on and we sat around drinking coffee. I motioned to Ali that I wanted to go to my room. She followed me and we sat, as we always did, cross-legged on the floor but the chat I had been so looking forward to began as a stilted conversation. I asked how her mum, Rosemary, was. She said she was fine and thinking about me, that kind of thing. The air was thick with tension and I knew Ali was having trouble knowing what to say. To some extent, it made me feel like a leper. I wanted to scream that I was still me, I didn't need to be handled with kid gloves. I was hoping Ali realised I didn't want all the cottonwool people had wrapped me in. I say that without wanting to sound ungrateful because I knew in her own way, Ali, like Mum, Dad and my aunt, was just trying to comfort me. However, Ali was able to push aside those first few moment of awkwardness. She moved over to me, put her arms around me and told me to let it go. And let it go I did. I cried and cried and Ali cried along with me. It felt such a relief to be able to let it all out. I needed to release all that grief so I could fight back at the man who had done this. I hated the fact this stranger had been able to do this not only to me but to my family and friends. When I was able to calm myself down a little, Ali gave me another hug and asked: 'Do you feel better now, hon?' I just nodded my head.

'Good,' she said, 'because you've just completely soaked my top!'

We both started to giggle and it was good to hear my own laugh again. Mum heard the noise and put her head around the door. When she saw my face she said how good it was to see me smile again and started to cry all over again.

I felt much lighter as the four of us sat around having lunch. My throat was still so sore I couldn't eat but Mum made me some soup which I managed to get down. A couple of hours later when Ali was ready to go, she asked if her mum could come into the flat when she arrived to pick her up. Ali and I love each other's mothers and Rosemary and my mum got on well. When Rosemary arrived, she didn't say anything at first and just held on to Mum and me. She said if we needed anything, she was there. They left promising to call the next day.

So there we were, Mum, me and Aunt Billie. We really didn't know what to do next. There had been so many calls from family that I said I thought it would be best if Mum returned all the calls and I would go and lie down. I headed into my bedroom but when I was by myself, I felt so lost. No-one tells you what to do after something like this, you don't know how to behave. Part of me wanted to pull the curtains and curl up in my bed with the covers pulled over my head and another part of me wanted to continue with life as it used to be—like going for a walk on the beach or seeing friends or doing those normal things. I couldn't leave the flat because I knew I wasn't ready but I desperately wanted to do something I had control over. I sat on my bed and looked out the window, listening to Mum talking on the telephone. It's pretty much what I was still doing when Dad came home at six o'clock.

It was strange when we all sat down to dinner. The conversation didn't flow and it seemed as if we had to try to find things to talk about. Mum and I brought Dad up to date with the visit to the police station and told him about Ali and Rosemary's visit. While the others ate, I drank honey and lemon drinks Mum had made to soothe my throat. I felt myself becoming lethargic and after dinner, Mum helped me to bed. I lay there staring at the ceiling for a while but when my eyes finally closed, the vision of the man who had attacked me appeared. For another night, sleep was going to be a non-event. I tried to fight the nightmares but even thinking of happier times before I closed my eyes didn't work. When I did doze off, flashbacks to parts of the attack had me waking up in a panic, feeling fear and finding it hard to breathe. I must have woken up at least ten times that night. Each time I opened my eyes, Mum was there. Unable to sleep herself, she would hear me crying and fighting in my sleep and rush in to calm me. At one stage my dreams were so vivid that as Mum was trying to wake me, I thought she was the man and I struggled against her until she called out to me that it was her and I was safe. I dissolved into tears. Mum held me and slowly rocked me, trying to soothe me back into a calm state. When I finally fell into a deep sleep, it was through sheer exhaustion.

I woke early the next day and saw that Mum had fallen asleep beside me. I gently woke her and told her I was OK and she should go back to her bed. I told her I was going back to sleep so she would agree to go. I waited until I was sure she had fallen asleep in her own room before I got up and headed into the kitchen. I would have loved to have eaten some toast but my throat was still not up to it so I settled for a cup of tea. It was still only about 5.30 a.m. so I put the TV on, turned the volume down and sat in the lounge room, my feet tucked beneath me on the couch, watching the early morning cartoons on the local channel which comes out of Newcastle. I had been watching for only about half an hour when the six o'clock news bulletin came on. Over the last two days, the media had picked up on the attack and the subsequent manhunt for my attacker. The police had given them a copy of the Identikit picture which the TV station and the local newspaper had been running along with some details of the man, like the colour and make of his car and the distinctive crocheted blanket he carried in the car.

I wasn't really paying much attention to the news as the presenter ran through the line-up of stories that were going to be on that morning—until I heard the presenter say there had been a development in the attack on a schoolgirl. I looked up; not sure I had heard him correctly. I listened as he read the main story. In the following story, he said a man had been arrested in connection with the alleged sexual assault of a schoolgirl. I stared at the screen as he went on to say that police had surrounded a house at Forresters Beach on the Central Coast during the night and taken the man into custody.

I knew it was my case. The police had made good their promise—they had got him. I couldn't believe it. I quickly turned on the radio which was tuned into the local channel and waited for the six-thirty news to see if they could confirm the TV story. Sure enough, they were also reporting that a man had been arrested. I ran into Mum and Dad's room, waking them up to tell them what had happened. Mum rushed to wake Aunt Billie up.

We huddled around the TV for the seven o'clock news. It was the longest thirty minutes! Then bingo! When it came on the screen, the news report was the same as it had been an hour earlier. I looked at Mum and Dad and saw they were as stunned as I was. Mum raced to the phone and called the police. They told her that sure enough, they had arrested the man during the night. Of course, Mum wanted to know why they hadn't rung to tell us. The police said they had thought it was too early to call because they had hoped we were getting much needed sleep. The police explained the man would be appearing at Gosford Local Court in a few hours' time and asked us if we could go to the police station because there were a few more things they needed from me. I told Mum that was all right with me and we arranged to be there by ten o'clock that morning.

When she hung up the phone, the four of us were all walking in circles, between the kitchen and the lounge, quite stunned they had found him so quickly and finding it hard to comprehend. We were asking questions of each other like how do you suppose they found him? Where did they get him? And, most importantly, who was he? In between having showers and getting ready to go to the police station, we rang everyone we could think of to tell them the news. My own feelings were all over the place. In a way I felt such relief but I was also apprehensive about what to do now. I knew the ordeal was still far from over but I felt this was the start of being able to put it all behind me. How wrong I was.

Down at Gosford Police Station we were taken straight up to the detectives' room. As we stepped out of the lift, what struck us was how quiet it was. In the past couple of days, the office had been filled with police yet today there were just four officers there. One of them was Rick Ashton and he walked straight over to us, a huge grin on his face. Rick and I had developed a really close relationship built on respect and trust. He will probably not forgive me for saying this but he reminded me of a teddy bear with his shining brown eyes. He made me feel safe and protected. He held his arms wide, wrapped them around me and said: 'We got him, kiddo.'

I didn't know if I should have been jumping up and down or not and I told him that. Rick just nodded his head and said he understood but it was OK for me to be happy about the great result. We headed over to his desk and he explained that Brian and Michael and a few of the other detectives were across at the magistrate's court where the man was making his first appearance.

I asked Rick if he could tell me the name of the man who attacked me and for the first time, I heard it. Frederick Glen Many. I almost flinched as Rick said those three words. So, he was real, he existed, he even had a name now. I was still experiencing that 'other world' feeling, a feeling of being a bit removed from what was happening, as if it was all going on around me, but to be able to put a name to the man made it all seem more real. Mum was not so restrained. The name Fred Many to her just seemed like a stupid name and she told us that. Fred Many. She said she didn't know why but she kept thinking what a silly name for a man. Fred Many, Fred Many, Fred Many.

We asked Rick how they had caught him. The officer in charge of the investigation was Detective Senior Sergeant Tony Thorrington. He had decided to launch a series of appeals that were broadcast over radio, TV and in the newspapers for information after the attack. The police told us they had been contacted by the parents of two girls, aged nine and ten, who had gone to the same school together and lived near Saratoga on the Central Coast. They described an incident which was almost a carbon copy of mine —except, thank God, they had refused to get in the stranger's car. The friends had been walking home from the shops when a man pulled up in a white car and asked them for directions. The girls tried their best to tell him the way to where he wanted to go but he pretended he had trouble understanding, trying to entice them into the car and show him personally. The man told them if they did he would then drive them to their homes. Thankfully, the girls ran away. When they heard the description of the car and the man who attacked me on the radio, the girls thought it reminded them of their would-be abductor and told their parents. We were told that one of their fathers was a police officer. The description they eventually gave police fitted Many and his car to a T. The girls even managed to memorise a few letters on the licence plate.

The next step for the police was to obtain a computer printout of every white Galant registered in New South Wales and manually they went through it in mind-numbing detail, trying to match the car with an owner who was known to police. It was when the police did their routine check with the local parole officer that they hit pay dirt. The officer told Brian Collis that while no-one with a modus operandi (MO) for this kind of offence was reporting to him, there was one man who had recently got out of gaol living in the area who fitted the description. Fred Many. Initially the police were a bit doubtful it was Many because his criminal history involved stealing, armed robbery and heroin possession, not rape, abduction and attempted murder. Then the officer mentioned that Many had been a keen woodworker in prison and had made wooden cigarette cases and lighter holders he was proud of. The officer said Many carried one of each with him everywhere and his description of them matched mine exactly. The parole officer told them Many was living with his new bride, Lyndie Cashman, at Forresters Beach, a small beachside suburb between The Entrance and Terrigal. Another cross-reference on the registration printout revealed Ms Cashman owned a white Galant. It was about five o'clock on the Thursday by this time.

With the finger pointing at Many, who was known to be a dangerous offender, the local police called in the armed officers of the Tactical Response Group (TRG). About midnight, Thursday, they silently surrounded the small fibro cottage that Many and Ms Cashman had moved into only that day. The couple had been living with Ms Cashman's parents at nearby Saratoga, just streets away from where he tried to pick up the two young girls.

On their first night in their new house they were woken with a shock at about twelve-fifteen when the black-clad TRG officers broke open the front door using what was nicknamed 'The Door Key'—a mechanical device that thumped into the door with such force it broke the door open. The officers stormed into the house, finding the couple in bed. They got Many out of bed and up against a wall to make sure he was unarmed. When Brian Collis strolled in, Many was handcuffed and sitting on the bed. Ms Cashman, screaming in terror, was forced face down and naked to the floor. Her hands handcuffed behind her back. She told the police where to find the keys to her white Galant which was parked in front of the house. In the boot of the car Brian found my false fingernails inside the left-hand brake light, just as I had described. Unfortunately there was none of the other evidence to find— the crocheted rug, the cane cigarette box or my knapsack which I had left behind. Many had been able to destroy everything he thought was incrim-inating. What he never bargained on were the false fingernails or the set of my fingerprints which police also found when they dusted the boot lid for prints.

In the car on the way back to Gosford Police Station, Many remained tight-lipped. Brian asked him why as an armed robber, he had got involved with something like this and Many replied: 'I don't know.'

That morning down in the cells before he was taken to court Many had threatened the officers: 'I'm going to get youse.' It certainly wasn't the kind of threat the police were unfamiliar with.

After Rick finished explaining how they had caught Many, I was still feeling a bit shocked they had been able to do it so quickly and with such ease. I simply nodded my head and looked away. Mum asked if I would have to identify him in a line-up and Rick said no because they had enough evidence on him. I was so relieved. I had been afraid I would have to look at him again.

There was something Rick wanted me to do. The police had found about six fingernails in the boot and needed photographs of them laid on top of my own nails to show how they had fitted. As I picked them up to place them on my nails, I realised my hands were shaking badly. I was hit by the memory of that dark boot and the feeling of being trapped inside it. Luckily the photographer was very quick and the nails were soon back in a plastic bag.

The detectives' office was filling up with noise as Brian and Michael Upton and the other detectives returned from court. Many's appearance had been very brief. He hadn't even applied to be released on bail and was remanded in custody. I felt a huge relief. As in all sexual assault cases, the magistrate had banned the media from reporting not only my name but anything that would identify me. No-one would know who I was, which was a huge relief.

The police told me Many was being held in the cells beneath the police station and knowing he was so close shot shivers through my body. My first instinct was to get out of the building as soon as possible but I realised I was here, I was alive and he was behind bars and couldn't hurt me anymore. Mum had a different reaction. She wanted to rush downstairs, push people aside, tear down walls, break into his cell and rip his face off, choke him and spit on him. You name it, she wanted to do it to him.

We both took a deep breath and looked around the room. There was a different feel in the air, almost a party atmosphere. The detectives had been working around the clock since I turned up at the police station two days earlier and they needed to relax and let off steam. They were some of the most dedicated people we had ever met and we told them how grateful we were. They, in turn, told us how they respected our strength and courage. It was about lunchtime and a few of the detectives headed off to buy Kentucky Fried Chicken for us all. Dad had bought a couple of cartons of beer for the police because we wanted to show our appreciation and everyone around me was drinking and laughing, and joking. It had turned into a bit of a celebration.

However I still felt like a fish out of water, not knowing what to do. As a rape victim was I supposed to be a screaming heap on the floor, was I supposed to sit in the corner quietly, or was it OK just to behave normally? Was it OK to want to yell, laugh, or cry? As people cracked jokes, I wondered if it was all right to laugh or would that seem inappropriate? Would they question my claims as to what had happened to me if I laughed? Was I expected to hate men and want to run from every man near me? I was in an office full of male police detectives and I felt neither of those things. I was trying not to be so aware of my actions but had no idea of how to react to what was happening. There was this marvellous celebration going on in front of me. Even though I was happy Many had been caught, I couldn't bring myself to show much emotion about it. Not yet anyway. The celebration went on for another two hours and we swapped stories with the police, getting to know them as real people who had families like ours. It seemed to bond us together. We were real babes in the wood as far as the legal system was concerned. I doubt that Mum and Dad even had a parking ticket. The detectives explained how there would be a committal hearing when all the evidence would be presented to the court and the magistrate would decide whether there was enough evidence to commit Many to stand trial in the New South Wales Supreme Court. They had no doubt he would eventually face trial but explained that justice was a slow process and Many probably would not even face a committal until next year. I had an unrealistic impression of how quickly these things should take, thinking it would have happened almost immediately.

By 3.30 p.m. I was exhausted and looked over to Mum who was talking to Michael. She must have felt my eyes on her because she returned my gaze and her look changed from one of happiness and relief to one of concern. Mum could see I was feeling tired. I felt so guilty about putting Mum through all this, the strain was written all over her face. I wished I could have made everything that had happened disappear. Brian said he would keep in touch and let us know when the committal was. We thanked everyone again, said our goodbyes and left.

• • •

At home we turned on the evening news and there, to my horror, was a shot of Many. I hadn't expected it and the image hit me like a ton of bricks. He was being led handcuffed from a police car into a building. His face was only visible for a few seconds but I would have known it anywhere. He did look slightly different and I realised he had used the two days since hearing the news that his victim was still alive to change his appearance. He had cut his hair short and dyed it a darker brown. But that chin, those eyes, that face. It was him. Mum says that the moment she saw him on the TV news was when her complete all-consuming hatred for him was born.

We had another quiet evening at home. A kind of peaceful feeling had returned. With Many in prison, I felt I could move on to healing myself. Mum rang all the family to update them on what had happened. The two of us didn't talk very much but we felt the need to be close. We still trailed each other from room to room around the house. After the excitement of the day, I felt weak and tired. I had a shower and my wounds still stung when the water hit my skin. The cuts all over my body were a constant reminder of what had happened. My legs resembled a spider's web and as the scabs were forming, the scratches were more noticeable. The same on my face and hands. Every time I looked in the mirror I was back in that clearing fearing there was no escape. The worst part was not the pain or the scarring, it was the look in Mum's eyes whenever she looked at me. I knew she could see the wounds and I wanted to cover them all up. After the shower, Mum bathed my legs in the bath with Dettol to stop any infection.

Once again, trying to sleep was useless and when the morning came, I felt that the days of jumping out of bed with a spring in my step were over. I looked at the sun streaming through the window and thought to myself that no longer would I plan a carefree day at the beach with friends.

Susie and Cathy came to visit and it was awful. They were trying so hard not to look at my wounds, to say the right thing but I felt like a sideshow attraction at the fairground, the type of thing that looks so ghastly you don't know what to say—like the woman with two heads or the apeman covered in hair. We talked about everything but the attack and I realised I needed to be back in the swing of things. The school holidays were coming to an end, I was due back at school on Monday and I felt like I needed some normality.

The weekend arrived and I started talking about school. Mum was worried I was taking things too fast and tried to convince me to wait a while before going back. Dad was home and things were very tense between him and Mum. They seemed distant towards each other and I couldn't help but feel it had something to do with me, that in some way I was responsible for whatever was going on between them. It was a very hard weekend. Mum had wrapped me in cottonwool since the attack and the more she treated me with kid gloves, the angrier I became. She constantly asked if I was all right, if there was anything I needed, if I was in any pain. I know it wasn't Mum I was angry at. I was angry with myself and the feeling of frustration but it didn't come out that way. On the Saturday night, Mum asked for the hundredth time if there was anything she could get me and I snapped back, saying I wasn't dead and that I could get something if I needed it.

The moment the words were out of my mouth I wanted to burst into tears. Here was Mum blaming herself for what happened and trying to do the best she could for me yet not knowing how. I rushed to her, threw my arms around her and cried into her shoulder, saying how sorry I was for putting her through this. She took me by the shoulders, held me away from her and told me in a loud voice not to ever say sorry again. She said this was not my fault and she understood how difficult it was for me. It was the first time Mum had ever really raised her voice at me and it did me good. Dad, noticing the turmoil I was in, piped up, saying: 'Come on, kid, how about we go out for a while?'

Mum looked at him a little surprised, her eyebrows raised quizzically but said nothing. I grabbed a jumper from my bedroom. I had no idea where we were going but Dad and I loved jumping in the car and driving around looking at the coast. At that moment, I couldn't get out of the flat quick enough.

Dad and I hadn't spoken about the attack at all, in fact, we hadn't spoken much at all. I didn't really know what to say to him. I felt I wasn't Daddy's little girl anymore, I had lost the role I used to fill. I felt my innocence had been stripped from me and there wasn't much I could share with Dad anymore. We headed south in silence, past Forresters Beach and the Terrigal turn-off with only the sound of the radio and the car engine for company. At the highway, Dad turned south for Sydney and it was only when we were on the highway that he spoke.

'I thought you needed to get away from all that at home,' was all he said. I told him that I had indeed needed some time to think. Dad was trying to act like nothing had happened but I felt I should say something. He had always been strong and I needed some of that strength. I wanted someone I could talk to about the attack without that person getting upset. However Dad didn't seem to pick this up and I didn't want to push it so we continued our drive in silence, a comfortable silence. We drove all the way to Wollongong, about as far south of Sydney as we lived north. Before we moved to the Central Coast, we always spent summers on the beaches around Wollongong. It was a familiar spot and looked pretty at night with the lights of the tankers out on the black ocean and the stars visible and bright in the sky without the glare of the Sydney lights to compete with. Dad managed to get me laughing about a few things. His brilliant impression of one of those elderly Sunday drivers set me giggling. We stopped at Austinmer and walked along the beach. It was about 9.30 p.m. and we had the sand all to ourselves. It was so good to feel the cool air against my skin and the wind in my hair again. There's a feeling of freedom you get only from walking on cool sand. When we started to feel chilly, we headed back to the car and drove to Kings Cross in Sydney which was the only place we could think of where there would be a McDonald's open. We ordered burgers and chips and I managed to get mine down, despite my sore throat.

Although Dad and I hadn't really talked much, I felt a few things had been dealt with. As we drove up the highway back home, I felt I was starting to get my life back into perspective.

CHAPTER 6

THE COMMITTAL

Monday morning just over a week later, I was putting on my school uniform ready to face the world again. Mum said she didn't think I was ready and she was probably right, as mums usually are. However after numerous discussions, she was persuaded to my way of thinking with the advice of family and friends. It would probably be good for me to have something to take my mind off the attack, was the way they invariably put it. As for me, I knew I had to get back to school to get my life back to normal. The police told us the committal hearing had been scheduled for March the following year which seemed an awfully long time away to us but that was how the legal system worked. School had already been back a week since the holidays ended and I didn't want to be left too far behind in my studies. I had received a lovely card from my English teacher, Mrs Green. She had written saying that I was in her thoughts and had included the results of an exam I had sat before the holidays. She had wanted me to know that I had scored really well.

As I pulled on the familiar brown and yellow uniform, it was quite an overwhelming experience. I felt so different to the girl who had taken it off just a few weeks earlier. I felt like a grown woman returning to the house where she had spent her childhood. I had a feeling of stepping into someone else's shoes. As we were heading into the summer months, we were wearing our summer uniform of short brown skirt and yellow short-sleeved blouse but that first morning, I wore my winter regulation trousers, even though they were really warm. I wanted to hide my wounds which were looking even more noticeable, scabbing over while they healed. I was very embarrassed by them.

Mum had taken the day off work in case I wanted to come home from school early and she insisted I let her drive me there. I was glad to accept her terms because I didn't think I could have taken the bus yet. On the way, Mum was concentrating on the road and trying not to look at the surrounding areas because the route to school was similar to the one I had taken on the day of the attack. I had arranged to meet some friends outside the main gate and Susie was waiting as we pulled over to the kerb. Just as I was about to get out of the car, Mum grabbed my right hand and held it tightly with both hands. She said very quietly that she loved me and for me to call her at home if I needed her. For that split second I very nearly didn't get out of the car. Part of me wanted to stay wrapped in the wonderfully secure invisible blanket Mum had had me wrapped in for the past two weeks. I looked out through the window and saw Susie and the other familiar faces and knew I had to go and get back to normal. Mum came around to the passenger door and hugged Susie and me, asking Susie to look after me. Susie said she would and that everyone would be there for me. Her promise seemed to make Mum feel better and she said goodbye. I headed up the footpath through the school grounds and looked back to see Mum just standing by the gate watching me. I waved to her and could see tears in her eyes. Quickly I turned and looked forward to stop myself from crying.

My day got worse. I felt like I had a spotlight on me. Everywhere I went I felt eyes boring into me. As I walked along the corridors, kids I didn't even know would be pointing me out. At that age, kids don't know how to be discreet so their interest was like a slap in the face. Even the teachers couldn't help themselves. I would notice them looking at me and talking quietly among themselves, trying not to stare. Luckily my class teachers were pretty terrific. Some acted as if nothing had happened and others, like Mrs Green and my history teacher, Miss Woodard, approached me either before or after the class and very quietly welcomed me back.

I couldn't understand how everyone knew what had happened. My name hadn't been in the papers, but it must have been that small, close knit community thing. Word had spread like wildfire and those who didn't know who I was in the morning certainly would have known who I was by the end of that first day back at school.

In the canteen at lunchtime, I waited for ages in the queue to buy a drink because there were only three canteen ladies on that day. When it was my turn, the lady who asked me what I wanted was the mother of a friend. We knew of each other rather than knowing each other well. As she looked at me, her jaw seemed to drop a little and a tear came to her eyes.

'You poor dear, how are you?' she asked.

I went to answer but another of the ladies came up to the counter and said: 'It's you, isn't it? You're the one?'

It left me feeling weak at the knees. I couldn't believe this was how I was to be identified, with this label that I was 'the one' who had been raped. I was still me, trying desperately to be me. I didn't know where to turn or how to handle this situation. I managed to nod my head and ask for a chocolate milk. I handed over my money and walked out of that canteen feeling all eyes on my back.

I joined my group of girlfriends on the benches where we always sat, outside the front of the school building. We were a pretty close group although not above the petty bickering that goes on among friends occasionally. I hoped being with them would take my mind off everyone's strange, intrusive behaviour but as they were friends, they had no qualms asking about what had happened to me. I tried to answer them and get it over with but their questions seemed never ending. Susie and Cathy were in this group and had been bombarded with the same questions during the week I had been away at home.

Despite the constant whispering and the finger pointing, being back at school was initially the release I had hoped it would be. I again had a purpose, a routine. There were classes to go to, text books to be read and homework to do. When Mum met me at the school gate that afternoon, I was happy to be able to tell her about my day and to have something to talk about again that was not Many, not the police and not the attack.

Softly softly, things began to get back to normal. I tried hard not to let things get to me but the everyday things I used to do, like going to Terrigal or catching buses, turned out to be a huge effort. The weekend before I went back to school, Mum had let me go to Susie's house for a visit. I was feeling confident and Mum dropped me off with Susie and her mum, Helen. I explained to Susie and her mum that I couldn't stay hidden forever and needed to start living as I had been before the attack. I wanted Susie to walk with me into Terrigal. Helen would OK it only after talking to Mum. It took a bit of convincing Mum over the phone but she finally gave her blessing so long as Susie stayed with me. It was a sunny Saturday afternoon and I knew Terrigal would be full of school friends and others I knew—intimidating but a great way to test the waters.

I wore a long-sleeved summer shirt and black leggings to cover the scars but the leggings were only three-quarter length and Susie was shocked when she saw the criss-crossing of scabs.

That day was very difficult but I felt the experience was worth it. I found myself slouching down as we walked and keeping my eyes on the pavement so as not to attract attention—nothing like the old me. The day passed in slow motion. We got drinks from the milkbar and sat on the beach for a while. We saw a girl from school, someone I got on well with. She was with her boyfriend. This was to be the first time I was faced with the reaction from a guy I knew and he was terrific, although I didn't know him all that well. He acted as if nothing had happened until Susie and I said we had to go. Then he came over to me and said that obviously he knew what had happened and if there was anything I needed to let him know. He was a keen and successful surfer and had won many surfing contests. He went on to say that a lot of the guys he surfed with passed on their support and best wishes. He added that they had all said that all they wanted was to get their hands on the man who did this to me. It came out sounding a little macho but I appreciated the sentiments.

Sometimes when I was out, I would suffer extreme panic attacks during which I felt the strength leaving my legs. These attacks happened if I felt someone walking too close to me or even if a friend raced up to me unexpectedly. One morning as I was walking to the bus stop on my way to school, a car pulled up along the kerb and stopped just in front of me. It was a completely innocent thing to do but I completely froze. Immediately my mind snapped back to the moment Many pulled up in his white car. It seemed that each time I relaxed, the tiniest incident would occur and wham! I was thrown back to that day. As a result, I never felt completely relaxed, just anticipating the next reminder.

The relationship between Mum and me continued to change. Like with Dad, I was no longer her little girl. She told me later that she had great respect for my courage and strength although sometimes she felt she no longer knew what I was thinking. At home we were still following each other around from room to room because we felt the need to be close.

Mum went back to work at the radio station but found it very difficult to concentrate. She said that while the attack was no longer in her face, it hung over like a cloud, muffling everything that went on around her. The relationship between Mum and Dad deteriorated to the point where they decided to separate and, of course, I felt I was to blame. I confessed how I felt to Mum and she convinced me that what had gone wrong between her and Dad had nothing to do with me.

Mum was the one who moved out because she was working in the city so it was easier for her to move there. She found a nice flat in Elizabeth Bay, the harbourside suburb next to the sleazier Kings Cross, and wanted me to join her. For my part, I didn't want to change schools and I wanted to stay with my friends for a bit of stability. I couldn't face the upheaval of moving. As difficult as it was, we decided I would stay with Dad and see Mum on weekends. The day she left was awful. Mum and I cried every time we looked at each other yet Dad didn't appear to care one way or the other and it brought home to me the lack of love between them. The moment Mum pulled out of the driveway in the car, I felt a huge loss. Dad wasn't the sort of person who would sit and hug me and stroke my head for hours like Mum had. After I waved her off, I sat on my bed and thought about all the changes to my life since that moment I got into Fred Many's car, and how I hated him for what he had done to my family. I vowed I would never again allow anything to happen to me that was so out of my control.

As for Mum, she saw this as a numb period in her life. She said it was like we were normal, but at the same time we were not normal. She said she would eat and sleep and talk automatically. Mum would go about her daily duties in a robotic way, but realised as we all did that we were no longer the people we once had been. Our view on life was now tainted, the reality of what had happened was always on our minds, we just couldn't function the way we usually did. It was as if we were on auto-pilot.

At school, I was surprised that I remained the local news story and people continued to want to know the nitty-gritty about everything. I refused to talk about it and tried to play down the situation as much as possible. At the same time, I was having trouble getting used to Mum not being at home and having to face the finger pointing without her love and encouragement on tap as it had been. We spoke daily on the phone but it was not the same.

I was learning a lot very quickly about human nature. The friends I had at the time I thought were true friends, who would be with me always, but at that age, or perhaps at any age, it is hard to differentiate between a true, sincere friend and someone who merely enjoys a degree of attention. Two of my 'friends' brought that home to me and forced me to make a decision I would not normally have made.

I had been back at school for about six weeks. During this time Dad and I had moved into the new house we had been building at Terrigal. The packing and unpacking had kept me busy yet the gossip surrounding me at school was still quite a drawcard for some people. At times, I would be sitting in class and have to ask to be excused so I could race to the toilets to get away from the prying eyes. I used to be the clown at school, the funny one without a care in the world, yet here I was on the floor of the girls' toilets crying, feeling so alone and out of place. It was like being an alien. I had started to dread the lunchbreaks because they gave people more time to point at me. I felt I was taken for a fool by people who would approach, pretending to be a friend when all they wanted was to hear details they could take back to others. I was feeling really low, like I had been swallowed up by all that had happened and there was only a shadow of me left. Then came the final straw.

I guess Susie had been feeling a bit like a star because she was the one I had been with on the day of the attack. She had always been the one the other girls picked on. Now they all wanted to talk to her and I guess she was feeling pretty important with all the attention. During one of those dreaded lunchbreaks, I was walking back to the spot where we all sat and saw all the girls in my group huddled around. They seemed intent on talking about something. My spirits lifted because I thought it was some new topic that had caught their interest. As I approached they all fell silent, a dead giveaway that something was not right. One of the girls, Sandra, turned and said the man who had attacked me had somehow passed a message to Susie saying he would get her because she was the one who helped police to find him. I knew this to be totally untrue but the gossip had already swept through the school. A wave of anger came over me and from the corner of my eye I saw Susie approaching from the canteen. I turned to her and yelled: 'Why, Susie, why?'

Susie didn't know what to say. She just stood and shrugged her shoulders. I looked around at the faces of the girls I thought were my friends and said: 'I don't believe this.' I turned to Susie. 'You know that isn't true, Susie, so why say it?'

Then from behind me I heard Sandra say: 'Oh come on, you've had your little publicity stunt, why don't you just forget it?'

I swung around, looking at her in disbelief but she just said: 'You heard.'

I asked her: 'Do you honestly think I enjoy having this sort of attention? Having everyone talking about me as if I am a piece of meat?'

With that, I pushed through them all and walked quickly to the headmaster's office. I wanted out, out of school and out of this whole situation. The headmaster wasn't there but my form master, Mr Andrews, was. I explained what had happened and asked if I could phone Dad. He led me into his office and as soon as I heard Dad's voice, I dissolved into tears. Dad said he would be there within twenty minutes. The last thing I wanted to do was go back into the schoolyard but I straightened my shoulders, held my head up and strode purposely towards the group. They stood around, waiting for me to say something but I just gathered up my bags and, looking at each of them in turn, I quietly said goodbye and walked back into the school building where I sat in the reception area waiting for Dad, wondering how my life had come to this.

A glint of light caught my eye and I looked up to see the sun reflecting off Dad's car as he pulled up at the gate. I ran over, jumped in and told him exactly what happened. He was very angry and asked if I wanted to go back to class. I thought about it for the rest of the day. I knew I would have to face not only the finger pointing but my friends as well. I didn't know how I could deal with them after they had treated me like that. I felt I had no alternative but to leave school. I knew it was going to make things harder for me in the future because I was only in Year 9 and I would have no Leaving Certificate. I also knew I would miss the general social side of things and the few true friends I had. I was surprised that Dad agreed with me but he said I had reached the right decision and he would arrange for me to go back the next day to finalise any paperwork with the headmaster.

The headmaster tried to convince me to stay when I handed him Dad's note informing them that I intended to leave and that I had his consent. We had a long talk about it and the headmaster could see there was not going to be a change of heart on my part. I had to get each of my teachers to sign my leaving form which was really awkward because they were teaching classes which I had to interrupt. I felt very self-conscious as I walked into each classroom and stood waiting for the signatures I needed because sitting at some of the desks were the girls who had upset me the day before.

My history teacher, Miss Woodard, was curious as to why I had decided to leave so suddenly and she asked me to step outside the room with her. I explained what had happened and she surprised me with her answer. She said she knew how awful the girls could be and understood how difficult it would have been for me to stay. She turned and headed back into the classroom to sign the form. Then with me standing there, she faced the class and told them I was leaving school. I saw some of the girls looked quite shocked. Miss Woodard went on to say how disappointed she was at the narrow-mindedness of some of the people in the school—and looked directly at the girls involved. Then she gave me a tight hug.

The form was completed by morning break and as I stood waiting for Dad to come and collect me, some of the girls from my group gathered around me asking me why I was leaving. I couldn't believe they couldn't work it out for themselves and told them to do just that.

After leaving school I had to figure out what to do to get my life back on track. A friend left a part-time job at a local fruit shop so I applied for the position. It was a pretty menial job but at least it kept me busy. I made some new friends who knew what had happened to me but dealt with it in a much more mature way than the girls at school had. Mum living in Sydney and working constantly and my workdays changing weekly made it difficult to get together. My home life became a mess. I was still having the occasional nightmares and panic attacks. Dad's work had taken a turn for the worse and he was often out of a job. He hit the single life with gusto and I hardly ever saw him at home. It meant I was pretty much left to myself which was really tough when I needed to talk to someone. I desperately needed reassurance that everything would be OK. There had been little contact from the police for some months and I was feeling as if the attack hadn't really happened yet here I was feeling scared and dirty. I think people forget how a rape can make you feel about yourself. Your view of the world can turn nasty and twisted and it is hard to remind yourself that not everyone is out there to hurt you.

It was almost impossible to grasp that this man who raped me had also tried to take my life.

The committal hearing was set for early March 1987. This date crept closer filling me with increasing dread. About a week before the hearing, Brian Collis got in touch and came to the house to explain what would happen. He asked me how I was going, and like a fool, I told him I was fine and prepared for whatever happened. Brian praised me for my strength and bravery. This was to be the expectation that would haunt me for years. I came to feel that because people, including Mum, had this opinion of me, then I had to live up to it. I felt to show weakness would let them all down.

Mum and I decided it was best for me to spend the week before the committal at her flat in Sydney. I needed a lot of time off work, so my employer said it would be better if I finished up there and I had to agree. I was very disappointed, because although working in a fruit shop wasn't fulfilling any ambition for me, I felt I was leading a normal life with normal demands. Once again I was forced into a situation where decisions, albeit it indirectly, were being made for me by Fred Many.

All the talk between Mum and me in the run-up to the committal was focused on expecting the worst—there would not be enough evidence to commit Many for trial allowing him to get away with raping me. Not that the word rape was ever used between Mum and me, we always called it the attack. The word 'rape' sounded so terrible and we couldn't cope with the images it conjured up.

The committal hearing was taking place at Gosford Local Court. A work friend of Mum's, Terry Gallagher, offered to drive us up there. He was a reporter and he had been covering the attack since it happened. He was really funny and kept us laughing almost all the way. Then about thirty minutes before Gosford, all conversation ended and we sat quietly with our own thoughts. Terry took us to the police station to meet up with the detectives but Brian and Michael Upton said they couldn't come with us because they had to escort Many into the courtroom. I just wanted to leave at that moment and head right back home. Without Brian and Michael beside me I felt I would be totally alone. However I stayed calm and showed no reaction—after all, they all expected me to be strong.

Mum, Terry and I drove to the court which was just around the corner. Gosford courthouse was a multi-level building. We found what level we needed from the directory in the foyer and got into this tiny lift. I felt chilled to the bone. Even though it was March, the day was very cloudy and matched just how I felt, cold and scared. Mum and I held hands while Terry tried to look at nothing in particular as he gave us some space for our thoughts. I watched the light on the lift's control panel rise to the floor we were heading for. The high-pitched chime indicated we had arrived and the doors opened noisily on to an open and barren floor with a few plants scattered around and a row of seats lined up against one wall. Dad was there waiting for us. I was surprised to see him there as I hadn't thought he would be able to make it.

A man in a dark suit approached us and introduced himself as the police prosecutor. He led us into one of the small rooms opening off the floor where he gently explained what would happen. He said he would be asking for what was called a 'closed court' which meant no-one other than the police directly involved with the case would be allowed in and the media could not report what happened in the courtroom. I was relieved there would be as few people as possible in court because it was hard enough for me to talk about the attack anyway without having to do it to a room full of people. However I did want Mum to be there and the only way she could get into the room was if she was a witness. So Mum quickly made a statement which basically only confirmed my date of birth and my age. On the statement Mum had to put her address and telephone number and she was so nervous she couldn't recall her telephone number and got the last digit wrong. The prosecutor said he would be calling Mum into the court first and then me. He said Fred Many was due to arrive soon and that it would be better for us to stay in this room until we were needed.

Sitting at the table in the middle of the room, I was wishing so hard that this could all be over. I felt so lost. Here I was a fifteen-year-old girl dealing with people aged thirty or over about something so personal and yet they seemed so blasé about it all. They were talking about court proceedings, which were so familiar to them but this was all foreign to me. I came so close to saying 'I can't do this' and running out of there but I sat still and told myself they were doing this for me, trying to ensure that this man would be convicted.

Suddenly a police officer burst into the room quickly closing the door behind him. He nodded to the prosecutor who explained that the detectives were bringing Many up in the lift. I heard the dim sound of the lift chime and felt a cold rush through my body. There was silence in the little room. A feeling of dread came over me as if it had drifted beneath the door. Mum and I were still holding hands and Dad was standing looking out the window.

I found out later that due to Many's criminal history, the police were taking no chances. He had already tried to escape from gaol a couple of times over the years. This time, police had handcuffed his hands to a huge heavy leather belt around his waist and had cleared the lifts and surrounding areas before bringing him up so no-one could get near him. He was rushed across the floor to the court and locked in the dock.

The prosecutor left us, saying a court officer would let us know when we were needed. It seemed the longest fifteen minutes of our lives before the door opened and the officer asked for Mum. Mum and I looked at each other and thought: This is it. Mum was shaking, both with pure hate and anger. I could see how hard it was for her and when she left, I had to sit in that little room wanting to be out there with her. I knew she would be looking at Many in court and I felt very embarrassed in a way, knowing that she knew what he had done to me.

When the door opened again, it was Sue from the police station. She explained she was here to give evidence but wanted to see me first. I jumped up and gave her a hug. She asked if I was OK and I tried hard to give a little smile but it was getting harder to keep up my brave face with my time in court getting nearer and I allowed a tear to fall. I was angry at myself because I felt Fred Many was winning so I straightened myself up saying I was fine. She seemed surprised but nodded her head in understanding. When she left, Terry had gone to make a telephone call and Dad had gone outside for a cigarette. Alone for the first time that day, I had a good cry. After about twenty minutes, Mum came back into the room but before we could speak, the court officer came for me. Mum grabbed my hands and told me to look at the judge and the judge only.

'He's right there, honey,' she said, referring to Many.

This was my first time in a courtroom and I had no idea of where to sit or what to do. Because it was a local court, it was a magistrate hearing the case and not a judge but at that time, they were all the same to Mum and me. The magistrate sat behind an elevated desk at one end of the room with a row of huge legal books to one side and heaps of paper on the desk in front of him. In front of the desk were two long tables facing each other. The lawyers sat here. On the left side of the room was another, much smaller, elevated area with a partition about chest height surrounding it. It was the dock and there, out of the corner of my eye, I could see a figure standing and just knew it was Many. The court officer directed me to another platform on the other side of the room, the witness stand, where I was asked to raise my right hand and place my left hand on the Bible and swear to tell the truth. The prosecutor stood and asked me to give my name for the record. The sound of his voice gave me a shock, shaking me into the real world. I had thought this would be the same as being questioned by the police who had done so with compassion and understanding, not with this booming voice in this direct and impersonal manner. I was totally unprepared and felt completely out of my depth.

I managed to give the court my name and the magistrate asked me to speak up because he couldn't hear me. I looked over at the magistrate and tried to raise my voice. The prosecutor asked me my birthday, where I lived, relatively harmless questions but ones to which I really didn't want to give answers because I didn't want Many to know anything about me. Yet there he was. I still hadn't looked directly at him but I could still see him out of the corner of my eye and I could feel his eyes drilling into me. It felt like he was raping me all over again.

The magistrate asked me to tell him about what had happened on the day of the attack. I snapped my head around to the right, and looked directly at him. No-one had told me I would have to repeat my police statement. Although it was a closed court there were still about fifteen people in the room. Of course I should have known I would have to give the details otherwise the court wouldn't know what had happened but I just hadn't thought it through and it took me by surprise. The prosecutor led me through it slowly by telling me to start with the time I left the beach, when I was approached by Many. When I got to the part where the car pulled up, the prosecutor asked if I could identify anyone in court as the man who had been driving that car.

At first I didn't want to look up and kept my head down yet part of me wanted to have a really good look at Many. The room was silent. I needed to be sure that the police had the right man. I took a deep breath and turned my head, looking over to where I knew him to be. I shivered when his eyes met mine. Yes, I knew completely that this was the man driving the car and I lifted my right arm, pointing directly at him. The faintest smile came to his lips and I felt like I wanted to vomit. I looked away, breaking the sight line that had connected the two of us for that moment.

I was wringing my hands as I looked at the prosecutor, waiting for the next question. He asked me to carry on with the details of what happened next and I went through the events of that afternoon and night as quickly as I could. The prosecutor finished his questioning and in my innocence I thought that was the end of my court appearance. I was just about to get up and move towards the door, when the other lawyer at one of the long tables stood up. He introduced himself as the defence counsel and said he had some questions for me. He asked if I had ever seen Many before the day of the attack and I answered no, with what I knew was a questioning look on my face. What a silly question! I looked over to Brian and Michael and they just nodded their heads imperceptibly, as if to indicate it was OK to answer the defence counsel. Many's lawyer then went on to ask me about the car Many had been driving that day. He showed me some photographs of a car and asked if I could identify the car in any of the photographs as being the car I saw that day. This was a little confusing because the photographs were of the back of a car and I hadn't really taken that much notice of the back of the car as Many was forcing me into the boot. I explained that to the lawyer, telling him that I was too afraid of what was going to happen to me as I was being forced into the boot to take much notice of that part of the car. I knew he was trying to get me to say it wasn't Many who gave me a lift that day and I was mistaken about the car. However I was certain it was the same car because some of the photographs were interior shots and even though the blanket had been removed from the front seat and the shelf under the glovebox was cleaned out, I could still recognise it as the car I had been in almost seven months earlier. After a few minutes of the defence lawyer shuffling through papers on his desk he said he had no further questions for me. The magistrate told me that I could leave. Keeping my head down and looking at the floor, I walked out of the room.

Mum was waiting for me and I raced into her waiting arms. We were standing in the waiting area outside the courtroom. One woman was staring at us and I started to feel really uncomfortable. I wondered if she had anything to do with Many and asked Mum if we could go back into the little room where I felt safer. After only another half an hour, the police and the prosecutor joined us to let us know that the magistrate had decided there was enough evidence to commit Many to stand trial. I was so relieved, Many could no longer walk the streets. All I wanted now was to put as much distance as possible between me and Many. I wanted to be out of the building away from the courtroom, the waiting area, the staring woman. I wanted to breathe the fresh air and leave all the memories of Many and the attack behind. The prosecutor was standing in front of the door and asked me to wait while the police led Many out of the court and back into the police cells.

When Mum, Dad, Terry and I were finally outside, Brian Collis appeared. With Many safely locked up in the police cells, he was able to congratulate us on the result.

'You got him, kiddo,' he said, giving me a hug. 'You can relax now. He's not getting away with this. It'll go to trial and that will be it.'

We wanted to know when the trial would be and Brian explained it was now a matter for the courts. He said it would probably be within the next year but could be up to two years. Mum, Dad, Terry and I headed to one of the local pubs for a drink. We didn't normally go to pubs but this was an out-of-the-ordinary situation and we had to unwind somehow. Dad ordered drinks for everyone, making sure Mum's drink was pretty strong. I sipped my orange juice and thought about the upcoming trial. For the first time that day I relaxed and I allowed myself to feel things were coming to an end. I believed Brian when he had said it was now just a matter of time until it was all over. Little did I know how wrong he could be. We couldn't even have guessed at what had been going on behind our backs.

CHAPTER 7

THE RAPIST

If there is one thing I have wished during this whole affair it is that I had never accepted the lift that day in 1986, that I had never climbed into that little white car. But what I have lived to regret even more is that the man who raped me was a career criminal. Why couldn't it have been someone who would have accepted their sentence, served their time and moved out of my life so I could peacefully rebuild my future? Instead, it was Frederick Glen Many, who had spent more years behind bars since the age of fifteen than outside them, who knew every trick in the proverbial book—who rubbed shoulders with some of the heaviest criminals in Australia. These were people I had only read about in newspaper headlines or seen on the evening television news, but because of Many, they were to play a crucial role in my future. When he attacked me, Fred Many was already living a lie. All things being fair, he should still have been in gaol.

Many had walked free from gaol forty-five days before the attack. He still had seven years, two months and seven days to serve of an accumulation of sentences which ran in total to twenty-two years and six months from December 1978. At the earliest, and with the benefit of the parole system, he should not have been released until 4 December 1988. But on 19 July 1986, he walked out of the prison gates on a special early release after going to the help of Peter Bruce, the superintendent of Goulburn Gaol, one of the toughest maximum security prisons in the country.

In March 1986, behind the walls of the gaol, Bruce was attacked with a knife by Raymond William Hornby, a hardened prisoner serving a life sentence for the murder of a flatmate. Many came to the rescue. Just happening to be in the right place at the right time, Many came up behind Hornby, grabbed him in a headlock, overpowered him and dragged him to the ground. Many, the 'hero', was credited with saving Peter Bruce's life. As a reward, Many was moved to the medium security Berrima Gaol in the New South Wales southern highlands, a much more pleasant place than Goulburn Gaol. Then came his biggest reward—his early release.

But Peter Bruce's life was never in danger and it was no accident Many was there to 'rescue' him. The attack was a stunt engineered by Many. On his release, he had confided in his wife, Lyndie Cashman, that it had all been a set-up to ensure his early release. Hornby later confirmed the story. In 1991 Hornby was back in gaol after committing another murder and was himself dying with AIDs. In August of that year, Hornby was taken from the exercise yard at Sydney's Long Bay Gaol under the guise of a legal visit but in fact he was taken for questioning by two police officers about a number of matters. They also asked him about what really happened with Peter Bruce. To protect themselves—or to shore up their own positions—the trend is for prisoners to write their own statements after such questioning and Hornby did just that. In his statement, Hornby said he told the police that Many had asked him to take part in the plan to take Peter Bruce hostage. The reason behind the set-up was that Many had been due for parole but knew that because of his unstable gaol record which included escape and attempting to escape, his parole would probably be denied. In return Many had promised to do what he could to help get Hornby out.

'I have never said anything in court about it because I thought I would be discriminated against by the penal system. Now I intend to tell the truth about the matter because I hope by telling the truth I will not be penalised in any way,' wrote Hornby, in capital letters which were designed to make the statement look more official because he did not have access to a computer. 'Everything written on this letter about the day's events are true and everything written about the facts concerning Fred Many are the true facts of what really did take place at Goulburn on 11 March 1986. I have not been forced in anyway to write the above, I have done it on my own free will.'

Hornby entrusted his statement to another prisoner and years later it was handed to a journalist, Janet Fife-Yeomans.

As it turned out, Many never kept his side of the bargain and Hornby was double-crossed. For Many, the ruse worked. He was released early and moved to the Central Coast with his young bride, Lyndie Cashman.

Lyndie had met Many at the age of fourteen through her sister, Julie Wright, better known as Julie Cashman. The Cashman family was notorious in its own way through Julie and her string of armed robberies. In 1983, Julie was Australia's most wanted woman after being sprung at gunpoint from a van taking her to prison. Her boyfriend, Bruce Kennedy, who had helped her hold up a supermarket when Julie was seven months pregnant, died in 1979 when he was hit by a car while running away from the police. Bruce had earlier helped Julie escape from Sydney's Mulawa Detention Centre. Then in 1984, her husband, Ray Wright, was shot dead during a payroll robbery at Wolston Park Hospital, near Ipswich in Queensland. The media reported the deaths, giving Julie the nickname 'Angel of Death'.

Like most schoolgirls, Lyndie wanted a penpal and it was Julie who suggested Many as a likely candidate. Julie knew of Many through Kennedy, who had met him in gaol. So at the age of fourteen, Lyndie started to write to Many. At the time, Lyndie was not unlike me to look at. She was young and blonde—she even came from the same part of New South Wales. Although Lyndie was the sister of one of Australia's best known female criminals, Lyndie never had anything to do with crime herself, although she is the first to admit that her association with criminals blunted her judgment when she met Many.

'At the time the Kennedys thought he was a nice bloke and I thought I was mixing with your average run-of-the-mill bank robber, which was all right. He wasn't a rapist or a sex offender,' says Lyndie.

'Being in gaol for armed robbery wasn't taboo. My sister was in for armed robbery and we didn't think she was horrible so anyone who did what she did was all right. It was in the days when we thought the crims were the hard-done-by ones.'

Many's birth certificate shows he was born on 23 November 1953, although he told Lyndie a ripping yarn about being born on 20 November on a boat which had taken three days to get to land to register his birth. He was actually born into a big family who lived out west in country New South Wales—a long way from the ocean. He always described himself as coming from Dutch descent and said his family name had originally been De Mani. By all accounts, he came from a decent family and none of his brothers and sisters were involved in crime. Many made up for them all.

He was committed to an institution at the age of fifteen and then sent to prison when he was eighteen, for stealing a car. He had since collected convictions for assault and robbery, stealing, escaping from lawful custody, possession of heroin, breaking, entering and stealing from a dwelling, armed robbery and further escapes from prison. To call his criminal record appalling is an understatement.

On 4 December 1978, at the age of twenty-five, he was convicted of six charges of armed robbery and sentenced to a maximum of eighteen years with a non-parole period set to expire on 4 June 1987. He escaped from custody and on 28 November 1980 was convicted of the escape and of stealing a car. He was gaoled for an extra eighteen months for the two charges, to run from the end of his previous eighteen years. He had the good fortune that the judge only imposed an extra three months minimum, so his non-parole period would end on 4 September 1987, the earliest date he could expect to be released.

Despite the judge's leniency, Many was back in court on 21 September

1984 and charged with conspiracy to escape from lawful custody and attempting to escape from lawful custody. On each charge he was sentenced to three years' gaol to be served concurrently and to begin at the end of the sentences he was then serving. That added up to a head sentence of twenty-two-and-a-half years.

While in gaol, he gained the reputation of being a violent man who was a bit of a loner. In the perverse world of criminals, he commanded respect because of his outlandish behaviour. In the early 1980s Many was in Sydney's historic Parramatta Gaol during the time when there was a series of murders as two of the prison gangs fought over the gaol's heroin trade. Many was loosely affiliated with the gang called the Grim Reapers. Among its members was a man called Archie McCafferty. McCafferty was Australia's answer to Charles Manson and had led a group of young people on a killing spree, murdering three people before he was caught. The Reapers all carried gaol tattoos of the grim reaper, but Many refused to have one—because they hurt. He knew because he already had two tattoos, one on each arm. One was 'Sue' and the other 'Shaun' although he would never tell Lyndie who they were.

During his time in Parramatta, a prisoner, Edward Lloyd was stabbed to death in the gaol and Many was to give key evidence in court against McCafferty and another prisoner, Kevin Gallagher. Many's evidence helped convict Gallagher of murder and McCafferty of manslaughter. It was an event which was later to become significant. He was also involved in the careful planning of an ambitious escape for which guns and gelignite were smuggled into the prison. It was all going to run smoothly—until Many was put in charge of the gelignite. Instead of using it to blow them all out, Many announced he was going to tape it to his body and threaten the prison guards he would blow them all up if they did not open the prison gates for him and his prison mates. One of the would-be escapees decided he was more terrified of Many than he was excited about getting out of gaol. He informed on them all to the authorities. When Many's cell was raided at 4 o'clock the next morning, the gelignite was found hidden in his bunk.

This was the man Lyndie Cashman spent every weekend of her precious teenage years visiting in gaols around New South Wales.

'I believe in brainwashing. My Dad said Many had me brainwashed and I think I was. I can understand how people get led astray. I was young and impressionable and he knew the things young girls like to hear. He would tell me I was pretty and the only girl in the world for him. He swept me off my feet but he would say to me, "Don't ever leave me or I'll get you",' says Lyndie.

She even agreed to help him escape.

'He played the "if" card. He said if I loved him, I would show him,' says Lyndie. Many was in Parklea Gaol at the time. He pretended to be ill so he would be taken to nearby Blacktown Hospital where Lyndie was to burst in with a sawn-off shotgun.

'I lost two stone worrying about it. He assured me it would be all right,' she says.

He warned her not to stand near the prison officers or they would snatch her gun from her but when she burst into the hospital ward, waving the shotgun, she was so terrified and overwhelmed by what she was doing that she deliberately went close to one of the guards so they grabbed her gun. She was sentenced to four years' gaol and served ten months.

They later married in Goulburn Gaol in 1985 against her family's wishes, not long before the 'hostage' bid involving Peter Bruce was staged. Like most other gaol romances, she was caught up in the excitement of it all and admits she was naïve and gullible. Also like other gaol romances the only contact she had with Many was a few hours each weekend. She was never going to get to see his bad side because he was always on his best behaviour. As for Many, he had little else to do but write her long, loving letters and send her beautiful pictures, always of naked women he said he had drawn for her in his prison cell. Lyndie saw the same pictures in magazines and realised he had traced them.

'He was a born liar. Fancy lying about that! He would also give me little wooden statues he said he had made, then I saw them in the prison shop and realised he had bought them,' she says.

But Many had a more chilling secret. He had a fetish for young girls, cutting photographs of them out of magazines. Lyndie also confided that Many liked her to shave off her pubic hair because it turned him on by making him think she was even younger than she was.

'I don't know why I married him. He had proposed to me very early on in our relationship and my Dad wouldn't let me marry him. I think that had a lot to do with it. He was forever writing me long, romantic letters saying he loved me and would be home soon and then he could look after me. He bullshitted me that he had a house in Manly (a Sydney beachside suburb),' said Lyndie.

But the reality of life was very different when Many eventually got out of gaol. The couple lived with Lyndie's mum at her parents' house on the New South Wales Central Coast. Lyndie was working on the checkout at the local K-mart supermarket at Bay Village at nearby Bateau Bay. It meant Many was by himself all day, often driving around the streets of the Central Coast and Sydney alone in Lyndie's car—the Galant. He was very possessive and almost every night would be waiting for his wife when she finished work. A young woman who gets on well with most people, Lyndie loves to chat but Many figured that when she was talking to the customers, she was really chatting them up and would grab her by the arm and drag her to the car.

'He never hit me but he was really aggressive,' she said.

Then came the evening he picked her up from work and said he had 'terrible news'. It was 2 September 1986. He told Lyndie he had been robbing a house to steal furniture for the rented home they planned to move into but the elderly owners had come home and he had had to kill them. He said he had managed to bury the man but had to go back and bury the woman. He collected a shovel and left. When he got home later that night, he was in a panic. He said that the body of the woman had gone.

'I cooked him dinner and we were romantic and whatever. It sounds bizarre now but you are not sure who is going to be next. Just because I was married to him, didn't mean he wouldn't put me in the plot next to them.'

Then he told her he had to get away from the Central Coast and left for

Sydney where he went to the home of one of his other women. Robyn had met Many in 1981 through gaol and a relationship developed. Robyn, a barmaid, had been swayed by the Many charm. While Lyndie knew about this other woman who was always in the background, she had no idea they had been conducting an affair during 1986 in those forty-five days Many had been out of gaol. They had even booked into a motel on the Central Coast as Mr and Mrs Many.

Back on the Central Coast, Lyndie heard the radio reports on 3 September about the attack on me and couldn't believe her ears when she heard the description of the car and its contents. She recognised her own car. She knew who her husband was staying with in Sydney and drove down to confront Many. She delivered the ultimatum that if he was innocent then he had no reason to fear returning home. Many told her he really was innocent —but asked her to wash the car, wipe it out and burn the contents including the cushions and the distinctive crocheted blanket. It was a very difficult time for her. Lyndie had just found out she was pregnant and the next day they moved into their rented home at Hopetoun Street, Forresters Beach.

On 4 September, the Manys' first night in the new house, Many was arrested for rape and attempted murder. Lyndie realised it was me and not this fictitious elderly woman Many had gone back to bury. Lyndie stood by him because he was still her husband. That first time she saw him in the gaol visiting room after the arrest, Robyn was sitting next to him.

'He had this stupid "what have they done to me" sorry look on his face. Deep down I knew what he had done but I thought, I'm still married to him and I'd better see what he has to say for himself.' She continued to visit him in gaol where he continued to deny the rape, telling her he was going to get off because he was 'doing a deal'. 'I'll be home soon. I'll get off this rape thing and don't worry, we'll do a deal,' Many told his wife. He would tell her over the phone from gaol that she shouldn't worry because he would be getting some money from the authorities and the pair of them would be given new identities and be able to start a new life. With the charges against him, Lyndie was surprised to find that in gaol they were left unsupervised and able to have sex in one of the visiting rooms.

'It was a little brown room with a sliding door. There would be a kick on the door when the officers were coming back so Many would know his time was up.'

But she had had enough of him. Lyndie had an abortion but told Many she had suffered a miscarriage. She was admitted to hospital suffering a breakdown. The last time she saw him was 14 November 1986, a week later she rang and told him she did not want to have any more to do with him.

'I didn't want him to have any connection with me at all,' she says. She divorced him as soon as she could and was luckily young enough to pick up the pieces of her life. Lyndie has since remarried, to a hard-working and very caring man and taken her new husband's surname.

As for Many, as soon as the prison gates had slammed behind him, his survival instinct kicked in and he lost no time in beginning to orchestrate his release. The only true thing he told Lyndie about the whole episode was that he had indeed 'done a deal'. The man who, unwittingly, was to help him do that deal had joined Many in Long Bay Gaol. In October 1986, Tom Domican ('Tough Tom'), referred to by the media as one of those 'Sydney identities', was charged with the attempted murder of Christopher Dale Flannery, his wife, Kath, and their ten-year-old daughter, outside their Sydney home. Flannery, a feared contract hitman with the nickname 'Rentakill', went missing on 9 May 1985. Flannery has never been found. Several years after his disappearance, the coroner has ruled he is dead. It was alleged that Domican shot at the family in the driveway of their home in January 1985 at the bidding of another criminal when Sydney's notorious gang wars over the multi-million-dollar underworld drug dealerships were at their height. Domican was refused bail and remanded in custody.

Many had seen his saviour, Tom Domican. Domican is a tough Irish migrant. Born in Dublin, he worked as a nightclub bouncer in London before coming to Australia in 1968, becoming involved with the union movement. He got a job on the Sydney waterfront and was an official with the New South Wales Builders Labourers Federation. Domican, stocky, balding and a fitness freak, is a man still in peak physical condition. He still teaches self-defence and fitness classes. Before he met Many in gaol, Domican was best known for being a Labor Party numbers man—described in the New South Wales Parliament in 1982 as an enforcer. He was charged in 1980 over the infamous Enmore Conspiracy, the alleged conspiracy to gain control of the Enmore Australian Labor Party branch by falsifying voting records. The charges were dismissed. Domican describes himself as a man of morals and old-style ethics. 'I never belt a child, a lady or an old man,' he told one reporter. He was also a man in whom both the New South Wales Police and National Crime Authority shared an intense interest during the bloody years of Sydney's gang wars. Domican always denied any involvement.

By this time, Many had become frustrated with a number of police officers he knew from around the traps because he could not get them interested in his case. He was held at the 'Programmes Unit' of the drab Metropolitan Remand Centre at Long Bay Gaol—the protected area of the gaol where sex offenders and informers, or 'rock spiders' and 'dogs' in gaol-speak, were kept separate from the main prison population for their own safety.

In mid-November 1986, Many asked a detective whose name had been mentioned to him, Detective Sergeant John Davidson, to investigate the charges against him. In return, he promised to give information about Domican. Even though Many was held in the unit, he claimed he was able to talk to Domican and other prisoners through the partition that separated the main part of the gaol and the protected unit. Many claimed it was through this partition that he and Domican had many conversations where Domican trusted him with all sorts of information. Many claimed Domican had confessed that he had been the man who shot at Flannery. Interestingly, Lyndie Cashman years later revealed that late in October or early November of 1986, Many had asked her to go to Gosford Library and look through newspaper files to find out all she could about Domican, Flannery, a Peter Drummond and the Seychelles. At the time she did not realise the significance but it appears as if Many was looking for as much information as he could to prepare his testimony for the police.

Detective Davidson was pleased to get some information on Domican and thought that perhaps, just perhaps, Many was innocent of the offences he had been charged with. It was a significant—if fleeting—win for Many to have a senior detective look into his case to see if there were any flaws. But Detective Davidson had never been a pushover for criminals. A mountain of a man, he was one of the country's most experienced and toughest officers, noted for his garish suits, including a brilliant red one which he was not shy about wearing to court. Legend had it that he carried the handgun made famous by Clint Eastwood's movie cop, *Dirty Harry*—a Magnum. Known to his colleagues as Davo, Davidson was widely hated in the criminal fraternity.

In his cell, Many sat and wrote a long and detailed letter which he sent to Detective Davidson. His story was that he was innocent and had been set up for the rape and attack by a man called David Kelleher. Kelleher is one of those people the media likes to call a drug baron, a 'Mr Big' of the heroin trade. Incredibly wealthy through his illicit operations, in 1988 Kelleher became the first person in New South Wales to be gaoled for life for drug dealing after he was convicted of conspiring to import nine-and-a-half kilograms of heroin. Many claimed Kelleher had set him up because of a row over drugs. It was, as Detective Davidson later said, a wild and fanciful story. He knew Kelleher, knew he was an intelligent person and knew he would have had nothing to do with Many. The detective didn't believe a word of it and dismissed the story as a fairytale.

However Many's deal was 'if I'm helping you get Domican, you should be doing something for me' so Detective Davidson drove up to the Central Coast and spoke to Brian Collis who showed him the police brief of evidence against Many. As soon as he saw the evidence, including my statement and the photographs of my injuries, Detective Davidson felt Many had taken him for a fool. He was revolted by what he read. He later told the New South Wales Independent Commission Against Corruption (ICAC) when it was investigating the use of police informers in 1992 that he never doubted Many's guilt. However Many became very useful to the police. As a result of Many's information the charges against Tom Domican began flowing thick and fast.

In December 1986, Domican and fellow inmate Peter Drummond, a former mercenary who had allegedly been involved in an attempted coup in the Seychelles, were charged with conspiring to murder another inmate, Franciscus Vandenburg—and soliciting Many to do it. Vandenburg, who was in the Programmes Unit with Many, has since committed suicide. He was in gaol having been convicted of murdering Megan Kalajzich, the wife of the ex-millionaire Manly hotelier, Andrew Kalajzich. Many was the main witness against Domican and Drummond, claiming Domican had asked him to poison Vandenburg although the motive remained a puzzle and a problem for police—Domican didn't know Vandenburg or Kalajzich. Domican was also charged with conspiring to murder a former detective sergeant, Max Gudgeon, also an inmate at the time. It was alleged that Domican believed Gudgeon had got wind of the Vandenburg plot—and once again it was Many who was the main witness to more alleged gaol confessions from Domican. In February 1987, Domican was charged with murdering Flannery and dumping his body at sea. This time the charge was laid by the National Crime Authority (NCA) despite its knowledge of a confidential police murder/drug taskforce investigation into the Sydney underworld that not only concluded Domican had no involvement in Flannery's disappearance but that went on to name the men they believed were the real murderers. The NCA's charge was based solely on Many's claim that Domican had confessed to him yet again.

Almost immediately the benefits of this informing began to flow down to Many, including the conjugal visits with Lyndie Cashman. While conditions like extra telephone calls may not sound like much, a whisper outside can be a roar inside gaol. Many later claimed at ICAC's inquiry into the use of informers that gaining things in the prison system at the time never entered his head when he became an informer. That was patently rubbish—if you have twenty years to go, one extra telephone call a week takes on epic proportions.

ICAC found that Many gained benefits not available to other prisoners, partly because of his status as a protected prisoner and more significantly because he was about to give evidence in these several crucial cases. The NCA gave him an electronic keyboard. He was allowed extra telephone calls to Robyn and given unsupervised gaol visits with her. He was also allowed visits with other prisoners who were held elsewhere but whom he wanted to see. Those special visits with other prisoners were covered up by the prison authorities who categorised them in the public records as legitimate 'case visits' while in reality they were visits he should not have been allowed to have. He was also allowed to meet with one of the witnesses in one of the trials against Domican and discuss and compare evidence—strictly a complete no-no. At the beginning of 1988, when Many claimed he believed Robyn's life was in danger, the New South Wales Police gave him five hundred dollars to help relocate her.

But Frederick Glen Many's real reward was still to come.

CHAPTER 8

THE CONTRACT

It was late afternoon on Good Friday 1987, a couple of weeks after Fred Many had been committed to stand trial. Mum was working weekends at the radio station. She was taking the talkback calls on the open line for the on-air personalities as well as operating the busy switchboards when she took the call that was to change our lives. One of the callers asked for her by name.

'Speaking,' she answered in her efficient voice.

The man gave his name, said he was from the NCA and that he needed to see me. The switchboard was lighting up with other calls but with the mention of me, the man had Mum's complete attention. She asked him why.

'Do you know where your daughter is?' he asked, urgency creeping into his voice.

He put her on her guard. She felt very uneasy because she had no way of knowing if he was telling the truth about where he said he was from so she wasn't going to give much away.

Mum said as little as possible. She just said that yes, she did know where her daughter was, she had gone away with friends for the Easter break for a holiday. The man was insistent. He said he needed to speak to me, that it was vitally important and could Mum go straight away to the NCA building in the city. Mum remained suspicious and told him she was working but the man stressed it was urgent and said she needed to get to the NCA as quickly as possible. He told her it was a high security building and gave her instructions on how to get in when she arrived. Mum dropped everything. She told her co-worker on the switchboard that she had an important call and needed to go out. As the other person took over the calls Mum grabbed her bag, ran out of the building and jumped in a cab. She had no idea what she was getting into or what she was going to be told. She sat in the back of the cab, willing it to go faster, her fears growing with every minute it took her to get to NCA headquarters.

Once she got through security at the NCA building, she was met by an officer of the Australian Federal Police who introduced himself, leading her into a room where there were another couple of officers waiting, sat her down and started talking. He explained the Federal Police were investigating the drug trade within the prison system. They had been using telephone taps, taping the conversations between the prisoners and the outside world. The officers told Mum that one of those calls they listened to had been made by Fred Many and he had been putting out a murder contract on my life and Mum's life. Many had Mum's full name, her address and telephone number. The police had very strong fears for my safety and needed to know where I was. Mum now knew it was for real. Mum was frantic and desperate to either get to me or get me back. She told them everything, that I was on holiday in Queensland, who I was with. The police officers asked her to phone her sister Billie in Brisbane to let her know what was happening. Mum called Billie, explaining the situation, trying not to sound too dramatic or panicky. She told Aunt Billie that Fred Many was making a lot of trouble and was trying to find me and that the NCA may need Billie's help so could she stand by for more news.

As Mum was talking to Aunt Billie the police briefed Justice Stewart, then the head of the NCA. Justice Stewart told them to do whatever it took to keep us safe. The officers told Mum that it was probable that she and I would have to be looked after under witness protection for a while. It was something Mum had never heard of but she couldn't think of anything but my safety and didn't really take in much of what they said about it. The officers said they would make some inquiries and let her know what was to happen as soon as they could. They told Mum she could not return to live in her flat, because Many knew the address. She had to think of an alternative quickly and suggested her mother's house. They bundled Mum out of the building and into a car, taking her to her flat very quickly so she could pack a bag. There were four officers with her—all armed

When they arrived at the flat, one stayed with her while the others went in first to check it was safe. Mum was struck dumb by what was going on. Everything was happening so quickly. She threw a few things into a small bag, thinking it was just for a day or two while she stayed with Granny. Granny lived quite a distance from the city but the police drove her there and told her to wait until they contacted her. There was very little conversation. Everything was done with a calm yet increasing sense of urgency. Poor Granny. Mum couldn't tell her much because she didn't know much herself. She just had to put her trust in police officers she had never met until a few hours earlier. While she was waiting, my other aunt, Mum and Billie's younger sister, Maggie, arrived to see Granny. Mum explained the situation and the three of them sat next to the phone. The next four or five hours dragged by. When the phone eventually rang, Mum had the receiver in her hand before it had finished the first ring.

The NCA had decided they would handle it themselves and not get the state police involved, they didn't tell Mum the reason why. We learned later that the name of one corrupt New South Wales police officer had been mentioned in the telephone call as being willing to help organise the murder contract. It was terrifying.

The police decided the safest thing to do was to go to Queensland to get me and bring me back to Sydney. They wanted Mum to go with them for her own safety and to keep me calm when they broke the news to me. Even had they not invited Mum, they wouldn't have been able to hold her back.

That fiercely protective mothering instinct was coming out. They told her to sit tight and they would come and collect her.

Eventually a dark-coloured unmarked car pulled up and two detectives in dark suits arrived at the door of Granny's flat. My aunt was so suspicious of everyone that she refused to open the security door until they had produced their ID. She was still not convinced they could be trusted and as Mum was leaving with them, she took her in the kitchen where she grabbed a medium-sized carving knife from the bench and pressed it into Mum's hand. Mum put it into her bag.

Mum turned to look at Granny and my aunt as she drove away and remembers the great worry written all over their faces. Before she left, Mum, acting on the latest advice of the NCA, had asked my Aunt Billie to drive to where I was and pick me up, this would save precious time. Mum had also telephoned me.

I'd left early that morning to go camping at Surfers Paradise. As I travelled north I felt like a great weight had been lifted off my shoulders just by getting away from everything. It was hard being at home when everywhere I went around the area constantly reminded me of the journey with Many. There would be no memories to face every day, no panic attacks, nothing for a whole week. The people I was holidaying with were an older group of friends and their lack of interest in what had happened to me was refreshing. My friends were able to handle the situation much easier than my friends from school and seemed nonplussed when I would get a bit panicky when something reminded me of the attack. We had driven up to Surfers in convoy in a couple of cars and arrived late in the afternoon at the campsite we'd pre-booked. We unpacked and put up the tents. It was a part of a bigger caravan park not far from Jupiters Casino and once everything was set up, some of the group decided they would head off to the casino. I didn't fancy going to Jupiters, deciding to stay behind with the rest of the group.

We were sitting around the tents when the manager of the park came over and asked for me. He said there was a telephone call from my mum. I made a joke about being checked on by Mum. We all laughed as I followed him over to the office. As soon as I picked up the phone, I knew something was wrong, Mum's tone of voice gave it away. Instead of her normally cheerful chatter, she sounded strained although she was trying hard not to show it. I immediately asked her what was wrong but she said everything was fine, just fine. She said she was calling just to let me know she would be at my grandmother's for the night and would be there if I needed to call her. I thought something must be wrong with my beloved Granny but Mum said Granny was fine and that I shouldn't worry. She went on to tell me to be careful, that she loved me very much and that I should stay close by my friends. Her manner was very strange and I couldn't shake the feeling that despite her reassurances, something was very wrong. I could never have imagined what it turned out to be.

Later that evening, about eight o'clock, one of my friends came to my tent and said my aunt and uncle had arrived at the park. Aunt Billie and Uncle Greg lived just about forty-five minutes from Surfers. My aunt asked for me but my friend not realising I had not gone with the others to the casino told my aunt that's where I was. Aunt Billie had told her that if I returned before they got back, to tell me I should stay nearby. By this time, I was totally puzzled. I put my head on the shoulder of the girl nearest to me and said in a quiet voice: 'What the hell is going on? This is just too weird, something is happening.'

About fifteen minutes later a car pulled up and I heard my aunt's voice. I rushed out from the tent and asked her what was wrong. She tried her best to smile and said that when she and Greg heard I would be at the campsite, they decided to drive down so we could spend some time together. I thought it was a great idea. I had a wonderful close relationship with my aunt and I relaxed a little. The rest of the group returned from the casino and I introduced my aunt and uncle around. My friends told me that Aunt Billie had me paged at the casino and when they heard my name, they had gone to reception and told Billie and Greg I was back at the campsite. God, what a fiasco just to see me.

Aunt Billie and Uncle Greg wanted me to go out to dinner with them and I asked one of my friends, Adam, to come along. Adam had driven me up from the Central Coast and I thought it would be nice if he joined us for a meal. Uncle Greg drove us to a pizza restaurant that was right on the water, just outside of Surfers. All the way there, the two of them kept chatting away. Honestly, they never shut up. Wasn't the weather great. How was the campsite. What a top place Surfers was! When we got to the restaurant and were shown to our table, the chatter continued. Even as we ordered pizza and cokes, the two of them kept it up. It was becoming increasingly obvious that all this cheeriness was a front. My Aunt Billie is the only person I know who can out-talk Mum but usually the conversation comes easily. This night, my aunt and uncle were trying too hard to be happy and carefree. About halfway through the meal, I could see by my aunt's face that the pretence was fading. It was clear there was something on her mind. I looked her straight in the eye and asked her what was wrong. Then I looked at Uncle Greg and asked him what was going on. I said I needed to be told—whatever it was. They looked at each other then my aunt started to cry telling me I had to be strong and calm. She said the police had taken Mum to Granny's house. Alarm bells started ringing for me.

'God, what has happened?' I asked.

She told me what the NCA had told Mum about the police surveillance operation in the prisons uncovering the telephone call from Fred Many as he gave out details of Mum's address. She said he had ended the message with: 'That's where the daughter is. Get them.'

I looked at Aunt Billie and she must have seen that I couldn't take in what was happening. She went on to emphasise what had happened, to make me see it was really serious. She spoke very gently but firmly as she explained that a murder contract had been taken out on my life, that someone was being paid to kill Mum and me. I sat there as if turned to stone, half expecting the two of them to say they were only kidding but the look on their faces told me that this was no joke. I could not believe this was happening to my family. It was like a plot from a movie. These sorts of things didn't happen to real people, not people like us who did nothing wrong and who had nothing to do with criminals. We were just an ordinary family. We did not even have any enemies.

As it sank in, my first thought was of Mum and whether she was safe. Aunt Billie explained the police were with her and that yes, she was OK but that I was the main concern. I couldn't understand this because I thought that by being outside New South Wales I was safe but Aunt Billie said the police were taking the threat very seriously and that no chances could be taken. Aunt Billie and Uncle Greg had been sent to pick me up and take me back to their house where we had to wait until we heard from the police. I was still finding it hard to comprehend.

'So you are telling me that someone is out there right now looking for me so they can kill me?' I asked.

Aunt Billie looked at me, nodded her head once and said only one word: 'Yes.' I turned my head and looked out of the window where, in the light from the restaurants along the beach, I could see the dark waves breaking on the shore. They crashed down with a wonderful hushing noise that filled the night. I looked around at the faces in the restaurant, seeing couples happy and chatting and children with pizza all over their faces with looks of joy that I had once felt. Their worlds were still turning yet I felt mine had stopped. It was beyond belief that there was someone out there looking to kill me. Me, a fifteen-year-old girl who hadn't asked for any of this. I already knew what it was like to feel you are going to die when Many had his hands around my throat and while I thought he was safely locked away, he was still trying to kill me. I just could not believe it. Once again, I had lost control of my life. It was one of the first things that hit me as soon as Aunt Billie told me of the threat.

Uncle Greg waved for the bill and the four of us, including poor Adam who was totally shocked, headed back to the caravan site. Conversation was nil and the only sound was the hum of the car engine. Uncle Greg ran a couple of red lights but I didn't think too much of it. I was functioning on remote control.

Back at the campsite, Aunt Billie asked me to pack as quickly as I could. I told my friends that a death threat had been made against me. There was a sense of disbelief and fear. I could tell this was all too much for them to take in. It was hard enough for me to understand, never mind people who had nothing to do with it. I was crying as a few of the group came into my tent to say goodbye. The last thing I wanted to do was leave. I felt safe being up in Surfers with them because it was so far removed from the attack, from the Central Coast and from Sydney. I was also scared of putting them in danger.

After rushing the farewells, I climbed into the car. As Uncle Greg fired the engine of his Commodore, he pointed out that further up the road, not far from the entrance to the campsite, was a car parked on the opposite side of the road. It was facing in our direction. What drew his attention to it was that its engine was running and the parking lights were on but it wasn't moving. It was just sitting there. I was waving goodbye through the back window when Uncle Greg suddenly pulled away at great speed with a screech of tyres and no lights on. I swung my head around to the front windscreen to see what was happening as Uncle Greg yelled at me to keep my head down and lie flat on the seat. The urgency in his voice scared me and I did as I was told. As I lay down across the back seat, Aunt Billie looked back over her right shoulder through to the rear window.

'It's following,' she cried.

Uncle Greg shouted out for us to hang on tight. As he put his foot on the accelerator, I was thrown about in the back. I could feel the car was taking turns at great speed. I wanted to sit up and see what was going on but I stayed where I was. I brought my arms up around my face, covering my mouth, and screamed into my arms so no-one could hear me. I was desperately scared. I had visions of the other car pulling alongside and opening fire on us, killing not only me but my aunt and uncle as well. I wanted to jump out and run away. Once again I felt guilty, guilty of bringing this all down on my family through my own stupidity.

After about ten minutes of crazy driving, Uncle Greg slowed down and said it was all right for me to sit up. I looked around and the other car was nowhere to be seen. Uncle Greg had tried to see who was in the car as he passed it at the entrance to the campsite but the heavily tinted windows hid its occupants. He said that as we pulled out of the campsite, the other car had pulled away from the kerb, made a fast U-turn and started to follow us. It may all have been quite innocent but we were completely paranoid and Uncle Greg said he couldn't afford to have given them the benefit of the doubt. Fearing the worst, he had tried to lose them and had driven around the block a few times to make sure they couldn't follow us.

'I don't believe this is happening. He's in gaol, how can he organise something like this?' I said, shaking my head. I was so upset.

Aunt Billie reached around the back of her seat and held my hand tightly. She said everything would be OK and when we got back to her house, we would be able to find out a bit more about what was going on from Mum. Uncle Greg ran red lights and still sometimes doubled back to make sure we were not being followed. I sat in silence, my face in my hands. I had no idea of what was going to happen to me. I felt as if this was not really happening. It was that surreal feeling again. There was disbelief, then fear, then anger, then guilt and then the disbelief again.

Suddenly Aunt Billie called out: 'What's that?' as the interior of the car was illuminated by red and blue lights. Uncle Greg slowed down and pulled over to the side of the road. He said it was the police. Every terrible thing I could think of flew through my mind, that something had happened to Mum, that there was even more bad news. Uncle Greg told us both to be very quiet and not say a word as he rolled down the window. A car door slammed and footsteps approached the back of the car. The dark figure of a police officer in uniform walked along the side of our car. Through the open window, Uncle Greg asked him if there was a problem. The officer explained that a tail light was out. I could see my aunt getting annoyed at having been stopped for something as trivial as this. Uncle Greg gave her a look that said to hang in there and stay calm. Then the officer looked at the windscreen and said the rego was out of date. It had been due that month and we were already towards the end of the month. Uncle Greg looked at my aunt and then back at the officer and said that he had left the paperwork and money with my aunt to mail. She was very embarrassed and pulled the papers and cheque from her bag, saying she had completely forgotten and would send it off first thing in the morning. The officer gave her a stern warning, telling her he would make a note of it and would be checking in a few weeks' time to make sure it had been done. Judging by the look on her face, I could tell she wanted to lash out at him and tell him where he could put his warning but she stayed silent and only nodded her head. We sat there until the officer had headed back to his car and pulled away. My aunt and uncle were very angry at being stopped while they were trying to get me to safety.

'Don't they know that we're here doing their job for them and trying to keep her safe?' she said.

It was ten o'clock by the time we arrived at their house. I walked into what were familiar surroundings feeling as if it was my first time there. I felt different, as if this was not me walking into the house. The drive had really brought home the seriousness of the situation. I had no idea how to handle this but I could sense how worried my aunt and uncle were and tried not to make it worse by bursting into tears or panicking.

I sat down in the family room, my favourite part of the house. Aunt Billie made us all a coffee—coffee had become the drink I needed in times of stress. Uncle Greg went outside for a moment, leaving Aunt Billie and me alone. It was strange that although we were somewhere we felt safe, we were still talking in hushed tones. I wanted my aunt to go over again what she knew because I hadn't been able to take it all in at the restaurant. She repeated what she had been told by Mum. We were just waiting to hear from Mum to find out what to do next. I wanted to phone her but Aunt Billie said Mum had said she would get in touch when she could because she didn't know where she would be. There was nothing to do but sit and wait. After about an hour, I began to get restless and started pacing the floor. It was very frustrating not knowing what was happening. I went outside and stood in the cool air, breathing deeply and trying to get a handle on the situation. As I sat beneath the verandah that ran the length of the house, I heard a rustling sound and turned sharply, not knowing what to expect. There stood Uncle Greg. I hadn't realised that he had been walking around the outside of the house, checking that the area was secure. Their house was on a corner and surrounded by a six-foot fence with two entry gates. Uncle Greg had been making sure the gates were locked and that no-one was hiding inside the garden. He saw the startled look on my face and quickly said: 'It's OK Kir, it's just me.' I nodded and settled down on the bushman's chair just outside the front door. Greg was very much the strong silent type. He wasn't very tall but in a family where all the women are under five foot and four inches, he seemed tall to me. He was solidly built and standing next to him made you feel nothing could hurt you which was such a comfort to me that night. I sat there feeling totally lost and he came over, said nothing, just put his arms around me and held me tightly, making me feel protected. I kept my head down, buried in his shoulder. I asked him why this was happening to us and started to cry. When I looked up, I saw there were tears in his eyes as well. He sat down next to me and promised me that with him and Aunt Billie, nothing bad could happen.

'No-one is getting anywhere near you, Kirstyn, not if I can do anything about it,' he said. Because he was such a big man in my eyes, I believed him.

Aunt Billie joined us and my uncle went off on his security walk again. What stands out for me about Aunt Billie is how alike she and Mum are. Having her there that night was just like having Mum. She held me, telling me that she loved me and stroked my head just like Mum would do. She reminisced about how she used to help me get to sleep as a child when she looked after me when Mum was at work. In the middle of the fear we all felt, it was a treasured moment.

When the phone rang, we all sprang to attention. Uncle Greg called out that he would get it and after a few moments he came out saying it was Mum. I went to get the phone and talk to her but he said she had hung up but would be at the house in forty minutes. She had been calling from a little airstrip nearby. While we had been speeding around Surfers, Mum had been flying through the night from Sydney in a light plane.

When the police had picked her up from Granny's, they drove straight to Sydney's Mascot Airport where a small plane with room for only about half a dozen passengers was ready and waiting. The police drove straight on to the tarmac and almost ran with Mum from the car up the steps into the plane. As Mum strapped herself in, the plane was already taxiing into place ready for take-off. Mum was surrounded by couple of NCA officers, including the officer who had first contacted her, plus a new officer who said he was from the internal police investigations unit. Almost before the introductions were over they were in the air and heading north. As the plane droned on, the Federal officer started to explain to her what was going to happen after they met me at Aunt Billie's. He told her they felt we would be safer within the witness protection programme and explained what that involved. He told Mum we would be looked after by officers twenty-four hours a day, that we wouldn't be able to go home and she wouldn't be able to go back to work. Mum assumed it would be only for a day or two, just until they got all this sorted out. Mum was shellshocked. She understood the seriousness of it, that someone was out there trying to find us to kill us, but she still could not quite take it in. Once someone is in gaol, you think they are safely out of the way. This was not supposed to happen.

It wasn't until the plane got close to its destination that it fully hit home how serious the police were taking this. The pilot was also a police officer and as they started to descend to the airfield, he switched off all the lights, even the landing lights. The only illumination came from the pilot's control panel. The talking stopped and Mum thought that the pilot even turned off the engines because they seemed to coast almost silently down through the darkness to land.

When the plane came to a stop, there were no lights to be seen. It was dark and silent. There was an unmarked police car waiting for them. Not even its driver, a young constable, had been told what was going on. His orders were to meet the group at the airport and take them where they wanted to go. It was almost inconceivable they had been followed but on the way to Aunt Billie's, the car ran red lights, went the wrong way down one-way streets and doubled around blocks to make sure they were not being tailed. Unlike Uncle Greg, they were professionals at this kind of thing.

I was sitting in the family room with my aunt and uncle when we heard a car pull up in the street outside the house. I was up straight away and raced over to the front door. I was about to run outside when Greg called out for me to wait just in case it wasn't Mum. I looked at him and realised he was afraid it could be the start of the nightmare we had been talking about. Greg told me to stay where I was while he went outside to investigate. He turned off all the inside lights and turned on all the outside lights including the floodlights that lit up the gate. Aunt Billie and I sat there in the darkness listening as the car doors opened and closed, realising there was more than one person out there approaching the house. In a loud whisper, I urged Uncle Greg to be careful.

He walked up to the gate and stood there waiting. It was then we heard Mum's wonderful voice saying: 'It's me.'

The relief I felt upon seeing her as she ran up the path from the gate and into the house was unbelievable. I jumped up and ran into Mum's arms, we held each other close. The three police officers followed her into the house. Mum introduced them and she remembers me being angry with them because of the secrecy because I felt as if I had been kept in the dark yet it was my life that had been threatened. So as Aunt Billie made yet more coffee, we all sat down so the officers could explain everything from the beginning. After hearing the details of the murder contract, they said they had needed to speak to Mum as quickly as they could. They had contacted Brian Collis at Gosford Police Station who told them where she worked.

One of the detectives said the death threat was being taken very seriously and we would now be protected at all times. He mentioned witness protection and explained what it meant but like Mum, I thought it would be temporary. Never for a moment did I realise what it would really be like. The detective said that at that stage, their concern was for our immediate safety as they didn't know to what extent the men involved in the contract knew about our movements and whereabouts, which was why I had had to be taken away so quickly from the caravan park. Sitting there in a room so familiar to me with these strangers in front of me telling me what I was going to have to do with my life really got to me and I started shaking and crying. It was so totally overwhelming. It was the sort of thing that happened in the pages of crime stories.

As we sat there in a stunned silence, the detective said Mum and I would have to return to Sydney where we would be handed to the witness protection people or something they called SWOS, which we only knew was some highly trained arm of the police. The officers appeared very concerned at having been at my aunt and uncle's for so long, although they had only been there for fifteen minutes, and said we had to leave as soon as possible. We wouldn't be able to fly back to Sydney until the morning because of the Sydney airport curfew but they would take us to a motel. The officers explained to Billie and Greg that we probably wouldn't be in touch for a while and that if they had any problems, they should ring a particular Federal Police officer and he would give them information. Soon we were being shepherded out the door, saying teary farewells to my aunt and uncle and promising to get in touch as soon as possible.

The police took us to a motel about thirty minutes away where they got us a room and organised us some toasted sandwiches. They were the worst sandwiches we had ever tasted but we were so hungry by then that they went down well. There was a detective in the room on either side of us and we were told not to open the door to anyone, not that we needed to be told. We climbed into our single beds but sleep was a long time coming. Not only did Mum and I have lots to talk over, but the walls of the rooms were so thin that we could hear everything on either side. One of the things that has helped get Mum and me through all that happened has been our sense of humour; being able to laugh in times of stress and fear helped us keep a handle on things. When we heard the toilet flush on one side, Mum shouted out: 'We can hear you.'

The detective called back: 'I feel sorry for you two then because my snoring is enough to wake the dead.'

Then from the other side we heard the second officer call: 'Hey, I bet I can snore louder than you.'

The bantering carried on along the same vein for a few more minutes before one by one we all called out the goodnights to each other as on the *Waltons* TV show. You know how it goes, goodnight John Boy, goodnight Mary Lou. We did it complete with terrible American accents.

Then Mum and I talked on quietly for quite a while. Mum had brought me up to be polite and well mannered towards others and here we were trying hard to go through the motions and do just that. We were trying to be as little of a problem as possible to the police, trying hard not to be too upset and to keep up the appearance of being nice and flexible and going along with whatever they asked of us. We had been placed in a situation where we didn't want to be a burden and trying to be compliant gave us something to concentrate on. We were both known in our family for being easygoing and that is what we were trying to be with the police. We were following each other's lead as we had since the attack. If I thought Mum was handling it, then I would try to handle it. In the same way, if she saw I was able to cope, then she would try to do the same. It was pretty much how we functioned in the years to come.

Yet here we were in an anonymous motel room and a situation so far away from what our lives had been. In just a few short months we had lost everything that our lives had been about. We had lost that sense of not caring about tomorrow, that carefree feeling. But the worst thing was not knowing what was going to happen next. I wanted to refuse to acknowledge the threat and get on with my life. I felt that by ignoring it, then it was not really there. But the situation hadn't gone away when we woke at first light in the morning to one of the detectives knocking on the door and asking if he could organise some breakfast for us. As we got ready and packed our few things, Mum was being all motherly and concerned about me. By seven o'clock we were on our way back to the airfield.

The plane waiting for us was as small as the one Mum had flown up in the night before but this pilot was an older jovial man who made the flight back to Sydney as much fun as he could. The trip took about five hours but being a small plane, we were able to fly lower than the commercial airlines and the views were stunning. Once we left the suburbs behind, the pilot invited me up to the front to sit next to him in the cockpit. Being fifteen you are supposed to be cool about most things and feign indifference if you don't actually feel it—but sitting up the front with the pilot was the most exciting thing. I will never forget being able to look from left to right across the entire skyline. The pilot was cracking jokes a lot of the way and after a lot of convincing, I took the controls and he showed me how to keep the plane level by looking at the instruments and keeping the nose up. I was so pleased with myself that I called back to the detectives that they were lucky I liked them otherwise I would have flown the plane into a hill. They joked back, saying they would buy me some flowers when we landed if I got them back to Sydney alive. For a short time, the atmosphere was lighthearted and not as if all the cares of the world were on our shoulders.

The pilot took over and I climbed into the back next to Mum where, lulled by the vibration of the plane, I fell asleep with my head on her shoulder. I had all sorts of nightmares revolving around being besieged by gunmen and taken to a room and killed violently. I awoke with a shock when we hit some turbulence. We all held onto our seats, as if it would help, but we were soon through it and started to see the crowded houses in the outlying suburbs of Sydney.

Coming in for the landing meant coming back into reality for me. I knew that once we landed, everything would start up again and we would be back in the world of police and radios and fast cars. I hated the thought. I longed to be back with my friends in Surfers and wondered, yet again, why this was all happening to me and not to someone else, not that I would have wished it on anyone.

When we landed, we taxied to a quiet part of the airport where we were ushered off the plane and taken to a small and rather spartan office used by the police in one part of the airport. There, we were introduced to another two officers, one was a detective sergeant whose first name was Bill, and who was head of the witness protection scheme. The other was a detective introduced to us as John. The pair of them may have smiled and shook our hands but they still looked pretty tough. The officers who had been up to Queensland with us explained that Bill and John were with the witness protection programme which was run at that time by SWOS, which we were told stood for the Special Weapons and Operations Squad. This, we were to discover, was a very select group that operated under the utmost secrecy. The officers involved were considered to be the best in the force and also the most deceptive. One of their major strengths was that they could conduct their work without the knowledge of any outsiders, and that even included other police.

We said our goodbyes to the detectives who had been up to Queensland and whom we were so grateful to for acting so responsibly. I gave one of them a hug. Yet again I had come to trust someone just as they were leaving me. I felt as if I had been deserted. Mum and I knew we had to learn to trust someone else all over again and this time the people we had to trust were with the witness protection programme. We had been handed over to them for safe keeping and from the moment we said goodbye to the other officers, we were effectively taken out of circulation. We were headed off on a journey into the unknown.

CHAPTER 9

THE PROTECTION

I have to say that our first night officially in witness protection was spent in a pretty swish spot. John and Bill had driven us from the airport in an unmarked police car. Inside it had all the contraptions you would expect, like radios and scanners, but on the outside looked like any other ordinary car. Mum and I sat in the back while the officers were up the front. We chatted about what had happened but the officers said they would save the full explanations until they got us to this 'safehouse'. As we drove there, I wanted to look over my shoulder to see if anyone was following. I had become completely paranoid in what was not even twenty-four hours.

We had no idea what to expect and no idea where we were going as we drove some distance out of Sydney. The police car pulled up outside a serviced holiday apartment block which looked very comfortable. It had been chosen because it had lots of security with bars around the car parking area and entry to the building was with a special security card. We went up in the lift to the top floor and walked out to find ourselves in an apartment overlooking the beach. Mum and I sat at the breakfast bar and leaned on the bench as Bill made us all a coffee—that good old comforting coffee again. We were going to need it for what was to come. We carried the steaming coffee mugs through to the lounge room which ran off the kitchen and sat down on the couches. Bill and John then told us what was going to happen. The situation was grim to say the least.

First, we wanted to know all they knew about the murder contract and they were very open about giving us information. They told us the name of the man they believed had accepted the contract. They said it was Tom Domican. At the time, Mum and I didn't know the role Many was playing in Domican's trials but we had heard of him and of his fearsome reputation through news reports in the papers and on television. The moment we were told he was the 'hitman' after us, Mum and I were terrified of this man. We believed what the police told us. We believed a very hard, very heavy and obviously very capable criminal was on the lookout for me. As the realisation of the danger I was in sank in, I started to cry.

Years later we found out that there was never any evidence that he was involved. He has since denied it, claiming it was part of the vendetta against him and Many's plot to frame him.

Bill explained that we might have to be under protection for quite some time. Mum and I said we understood this and asked about what measures they would take to secure Mum's apartment at Elizabeth Bay so that we could stay there. The two detectives seemed quite surprised at this and looked at each other. John leaned forward and sat squarely in front of us.

'No, you don't understand. You will be staying here until we deem the threat to be over. At this stage we feel that the threat warrants you to be kept under extreme protection which means that we can't have you returning home just yet,' he said, in a kind but very firm tone.

Mum and I were shocked. Mum started to ask questions. What about her job? What about our family? What about her flat? What about her clothes and other things? I was too stunned to even say anything and just sat listening to the officers. They explained that originally, while they had thought the threat to be real, they had thought it would blow over. However since they had learned that it was Domican carrying out the hit, they felt it was important that we were as far away from our usual surroundings as possible. We were never going to be able to go home again, not even to pack up our belongings. They said they would be organising a removal van to clean out Mum's flat. Everything would be packed up and placed into storage.

It was at this stage that they first brought up the possibility of us changing our identities. Bill and John explained that in similar situations, people had to not only move away from where they were known but had to completely change their identities in order to live a safe life. They did say that they did not know at that stage whether this would be the case for us but they wanted us to realise it might well be a possibility. This was all too much for me. They may have put us in a plush apartment but they were about to make us strangers in our own lives.

I got up and walked into one of the bedrooms, closing the door behind me. I needed just a few moments by myself to come to terms with it all. I sat there on the bed looking at my hands and the scars which had been left all over my legs. I sat there trying to pull myself together. I knew it was pointless trying to fight this and I felt I owed it to Mum to try to cope as best I could. She had just been told that her life as she knew it was to be no more and I felt I had no right to be so selfish as to think only of myself and the effect this would have on me. Mum would now be away from her work that she loved so much, away from her friends, away from her beautiful home and basically away from anything normal at all. I straightened myself up and as I opened the door back into the lounge room, I heard Mum's voice raised in fear, asking how Many had managed to get her personal details.

They were discussing the telephone call Many had made from gaol in which he gave out Mum's details. Bill said it appeared the information had been gleaned from the last minute statement Mum had made outside the committal hearing because it had that same mistake of the last digit wrong. This was why the police internal affairs department had been involved because it was feared it was a police officer who had passed on Mum's details from her statement. This latest bombshell was the worst thing they could have told us because it then had us questioning the integrity of all the wonderful officers involved in our case back in Gosford. We were sure that none of those we had got to know so well would have put our lives at risk but it was awful to think that one of their colleagues may have done just that, and for what? Drugs, money, who knows? It was hard to know who to trust.

Bill announced that he had to leave. As head of the witness protection scheme, he had come along to introduce himself and to help settle us into it but he was now leaving us with John and another officer, called Mitch, who would be joining us soon. So there we were sitting with John in the lounge room overlooking the ocean, not knowing what to do with ourselves. John said he'd leave us some space to come to terms with the information we had been bombarded with. He gave us every number that we may need to contact him on; home phone, mobile and pager. He said we were not to answer the phone, go out or even open the door until he returned. He said he would pick up some groceries for us on the way back so we could stock up the fridge and Mum tried to give him some money. She was really embarrassed when he wouldn't take it. John was insistent—but then so was Mum. She just couldn't get her head around the idea of someone paying for something for us as basic as groceries. John explained that because of the situation we were in, the police were responsible for us and would be covering the costs incurred because of the need for protection. She finally had to give in and accept his insistence on paying for the food.

When the door slammed shut behind John, Mum and I were left staring at each other, not really knowing what to do. We tried to get settled by putting away our few things and to get some sort of order in our lives. It only took us a few minutes. That done, we sat out on the balcony with cups of coffee. I said to Mum that I couldn't believe this was happening. My overwhelming feeling was numbness, total numbness. Mum and I sat there suspended in time until John returned about an hour later, bringing the groceries and our new protector, Mitch. It was the two of them who would be looking after us, at least for the time being. Mum and I were so relieved to have something to do that we even enjoyed putting the groceries away—

that was how desperate we were. It was still only early afternoon and we spent the rest of the day getting to know each other.

The two of them were pretty casual in their manner and open in discussions with us. We got to know each other a bit, chatting about their families and where they lived. They asked about where we had come from. Any questions we had, they tried to answer as honestly as they could and we explained that by now, so much had happened to us that we could handle any news, no matter how grave. We just wanted to be told the truth. They explained the people they usually looked after in protection were criminals who had given evidence against their criminal mates. It was rare for innocent people like us to be caught up in all this. Mum and I have always thought that this was one of the major reasons why we were looked after so well.

As they relaxed, they took off their jackets and I was shocked to see they were wearing shoulder holsters carrying guns. Mitch asked if we would rather they took their guns off but we said it was something we would have to get used to so they might as well leave them on. John bent down to his ankle and removed a second gun he had there. Mum and I looked at each other, eyes wide open and raised our eyebrows at each other. Once again, it was like being part of a movie. John simply said his ankle gun was uncomfortable and put it on the kitchen bench.

The two officers were pretty relaxed around us, yet at the same time were very professional. We all got on well but we could only take so much of being cooped up. After a few days it started getting to Mum and me. I started to feel a little stir crazy. Being shut up in this apartment with two men we hardly knew was tough and added to that was the lack of privacy and the intrusion into our lives. We felt this desperate need to speak to our family and friends and after much pleading with John and Mitch, they finally allowed us to speak to Aunt Billie and to Granny. However it wasn't as simple as picking up the phone in the apartment and dialling them. We had to let John telephone a special number to a police switchboard which then transferred the call to another switchboard interstate which then switched the call to a different switchboard which then dialled the number we wanted.

We were then put on hold as they called the number and connected us through. John explained that doing it this way meant it was impossible for anyone to trace the call. An extreme measure but merited in the case of the extreme threat.

Hearing Aunt Billie's voice again was sheer delight. We had to speak quickly because Mitch told us we didn't have long. Mum spoke first and I could tell that my aunt had asked where we were. Mum was just about to tell her when John shook his head, signalling she couldn't reveal our location. Asking my aunt to hold on, Mum asked John what was wrong and he explained that no-one was to know where we were. At this point, Mum got upset.

'But she's my sister, who is she going to tell?' she said.

John said it was better for everyone to do it his way, so we found ourselves talking to relatives but not being able to say much at all. Mum tried to sound upbeat and light for my aunt and I did the same.

The days dragged by. Despite the tough talk of the police, Mum and I had thought it would all be over in a week but here we were still in the apartment, unable to leave and feeling caged up. We tried to find things to do. Mum even asked if she could go to a wool store and buy some wool so she could teach me how to knit. We decided we would try to knit one jumper each. I had to stay in the apartment while John accompanied Mum to the shops. It was pretty frightening watching John put his shoulder holster on. He had got into the habit of taking it off when he was inside the apartment with us and seeing him put it back on just to walk to the shops with Mum brought home to me how serious our situation was. With the wool we had something else to fill our time with—so our days consisted of knitting, reading and watching TV. Great.

Twenty-four hours a day, everything we wanted, everything we needed, almost our every thought, had to go through the police. If we wanted something personal from the chemist, if we wanted an ice cream, we had to ask John and Mitch. If we wanted to go for a walk on the beach, it had to be with their permission and they had to come with us. They were with us all day and at night slept in the apartment, which was tough for them with families at home. Mum and I began to resent, not the detectives as people, but the intrusion of them into our lives. We had no personal space. At one stage, Mum and I got very snappy with each other, very niggly. It didn't last long and happened in short bursts but it was something we had never done before.

We both resented that we had been put in this situation by Fred Many. I was really angry that I had put Mum and my family through this and I just wanted it all to go away. I felt real rage towards Many. He became enemy number one. I saw him as a person trying to again take away my life and also the lives of Mum and our family.

Yet it became harder and harder for me to show my feelings. I could see how concerned Mum and even the police were for me and I didn't want to add to their worries so I did my best to keep my emotions hidden. Many nights I heard Mum crying in her room and every time it broke my heart. I felt so responsible for her pain. I knew she was dealing with the guilt she felt for what had happened to me and to this day she still feels she was at fault, no matter how I try to convince her that it was my decision to get in the car that day, despite all her warnings.

Ten days into witness protection and our lives were turned upside down again when we were told we had to move out of the apartment and stay somewhere else for just one night. Our apartment had been booked by people using it for their holiday. There was an apartment on the other side of the block, facing the town, but it wouldn't be free until the next night. Although the sound of a move doesn't sound too strenuous, the upheaval was heartbreaking. We had to pack up again and were ushered out of the building like some dirty little secret. It was so deflating. It felt like we were being torn from what little security we had. Still, Mum and I did our best not to make too much of a fuss.

John explained they had another safehouse for us for that night, not far from the apartment. It turned out to be a one-bedroom flat but the worst part of it was that it was someone's home. The owners were overseas and had rented the flat to the police. We were installed there and told to relax. Mum and I nodded our heads and watched as John and Mitch left us to get some takeaway food for dinner. As we put our bags down, we looked at each other and knew we were both thinking the same thing—we felt as if we were trespassers. The flat was small and cluttered with the personal belongings of the owners. Their photos were on the walls and their ornaments on shelves and the top of a chest of drawers. I tried to find somewhere to put my luggage out of the way and opened a hall cupboard only to find personal towels and sheets. It was really upsetting to have to move around other people's possessions. It was awful.

John and Mitch arrived back with Kentucky Fried Chicken—being in witness protection was certainly no culinary delight—and said they would leave us for the night. They had no choice, as there was nowhere for them to sleep. They said to get in touch if we needed anything. Having finished dinner, Mum and I went into the kitchen to get a cup of coffee. We found the coffee cups had ring marks in them and the teaspoons were stained brown from coffee and tea. It wasn't that we didn't have those stains on our own cups and teaspoons at home, but knowing these stains belonged to someone else was hard to deal with. We simply ignored our need for a drink and spent the rest of the evening sitting precariously on the edge of the two-seater sofa watching TV and trying not to notice the crowds of personal effects that surrounded us. Our sense of dislodgement was only heightened by where we were and try as we might, this time we couldn't see the lighter side of things. Conversation between us was extremely stilted that night.

By midnight, we felt we should try to get some sleep. At least the morning would come quicker. We made sure the lounge room was spotless, not that it needed much cleaning as we hadn't dared touch anything. But on walking into the bedroom we knew there was no way we would be able to feel comfortable enough to sleep. This room was again filled with personal items down to hairpins on the dresser. Being in a stranger's house without having their direct permission to be there made us feel like thieves who had broken in during the night.

We quietly closed the bedroom door and went back to the lounge room. We moved the two armchairs in front of each other to make a bed for me while Mum lay down on the sofa. We realised we needed pillows but couldn't bring ourselves to go back into the bedroom to get them. It was so intrusive. We tried to sleep but it didn't happen. We felt silly feeling so uncomfortable in someone else's house but we could no longer fight the urge to leave and after an hour debating whether we should ring John and tell him, we finally called him. We were feeling very bad when he arrived at 2 a.m. to pick us up and did nothing but apologise to him over and over again. However he was just wonderful and said he could understand how we felt. He even went so far as to say that because we were the type of people we were, that he could understand our guilt at being in a stranger's home. He explained the only hotel in the area was quite rundown but by that time, Mum and I didn't care how bad it was just so long as it had rooms that had no-one's identity stamped on them. We pulled up at a tiny hotel just off the main road and, with sighs of relief, settled ourselves in.

Mitch came by at about 10.30 a.m. to take us back to the apartment overlooking the town. Installed back in the apartment block, we resumed our non-existent lives. Mum was missing work and I was missing family and friends. I very much wanted to talk to Dad which turned out to be a greater fiasco than it had been speaking to Aunt Billie and Granny. Again, the call was routed and rerouted through switchboard after switchboard until it got to the Terrigal Police Station where officers had to pick Dad up from our house and take him to the police station where I had to call all over again at a pre-arranged time. Unlike Mum and I, Dad seemed quite thrilled about what was going on and seemed excited as he told me about his dealings with the police and which detectives he had had drinks with recently.

The days dragged by. Each morning we woke with the realisation that neither of us had any tasks to do, telephone calls to make, people to meet. We didn't feel useful any longer, we felt empty and very alone. Our world was the apartment, the TV and a couple of police officers. John and Mitch had begun to leave us during the day to give us some privacy but we were still not allowed out without them.

For me, the evenings and nights were the worst. Being alone behind the shield of my bedroom door was partly a relief because there were times I needed to be by myself but it was during those times when I was alone that my mind became flooded with the face of Many and what had happened that night in the bush. I was feeling totally dislodged being in witness protection. All of a sudden, while still shellshocked from the attack, my life was ripped apart again. I had had no time to settle, to get comfortable with myself again. I knew Mum was just in the next room and that was comforting but trying to get through all this was too much for me. Night after night I would curl up beneath the quilt and cry myself to sleep. Nothing can prepare you for a situation like that when you are fifteen. Day to day, week by week our routine never changed—there was nothing to happen to change it.

One thing I did achieve was to persuade John to let me speak with my friends from the Central Coast who had been home from the Surfers holiday for weeks. I called my friend Adam because I knew it was his twenty-first birthday at the end of the week. It was so good to talk to someone who had a normal life outside our little quartet. He told me how everyone was going to his birthday—and how his family was organising a huge party at their home and he invited me to go. That was all I needed. Escape! All I wanted was one night with my friends, just one tiny taste of life to help me deal with being locked up in this apartment again. I waited patiently until after dinner that night and then took the plunge. I asked John if I could please, possibly, go to the party. In my naivety, I thought he would say sure, no problem but what he did say was no. A very firm no. He said it was impossible and that it was stupid for me to be anywhere near the Central Coast at this stage.

As far as I was concerned, his refusal was like a red rag to a bull. That was it. There was no way I was going to be dictated to and stopped from going to the party by Fred Many and I told John so. I also told him that if he didn't allow me to go, then I would simply walk out of the flat when he was not there, catch a country train to the coast and go to the party by myself. I burst into tears but stood there before him like a defiant child with no intention of budging. I felt this was a chance for me to take charge and make a decision about my life. I stood in the middle of the lounge room, feet apart, hands on hips and looked directly into John's eyes. I think he knew how determined I was and that no amount of reasoning was going to change my mind. I am sure he understood why I was being so feisty. He had been able to understand how hard the situation was for us. Mum, of course, had a totally different view. The look on her face when I first mentioned it said it all. While she understood my need to see my friends, she thought I must be losing my mind to even suggest actually doing such a thing.

John asked Mum if he could speak to her about it and this made me angrier.

'Why not speak to me about it, I'm part of all this too,' I said. Mum looked at me with a look that said 'don't be so rude, Kirstyn'. I knew I was difficult and a bit rude but my need to take control was overwhelming. So they discussed it in front of me and we compromised, leaving it up to John's superior which meant leaving it until the next day to get an answer. The anticipation. Finally John's boss came through and said it was OK for me to go on the condition that John and Mitch came with me. Mum was also coming but that was fine because she knew Adam and his family but I felt a bit disappointed that the police had to go to the party as well. John explained they had to drive us there and that I would be able to stay for a couple of hours only and for my own safety, I couldn't tell Adam I was going. Two hours was better than nothing. I called Adam, it was hard hearing the disappointment in his voice when I told him I couldn't make it—but I was excited about being able to surprise him.

The day of the party arrived and I started to feel a bit silly about having pushed it to the point of going because all day was spent listening to John and Mitch on the phone organising the trip with other police, including the local police at Terrigal. They wanted the Terrigal police to cruise around the area where Adam lived to make sure no-one suspicious was hanging around. They feared the people looking for us would know about my friendship with

Adam, hoping I would go to the party, something I hadn't thought about in my eagerness to go. I realised how much was at stake and how much of an effort it was for the police to try to protect us. It was a long drive but by 6.30 p.m. on the Saturday night we were getting close to the coast and in the back of the unmarked police car I was a bundle of nerves at being able to see all my friends again and step back into my normal life, even if it was only for an hour or two. Terrigal police had quietly surrounded the perimeter of Adam's house and were keeping a close eye on the area. Mitch constantly communicated with them over the radio. Of course Adam had no idea this was going on and I wondered how he would feel if he knew his home was staked out by the police.

When we pulled up outside, John, Mitch and I went to the rear of the car and opened the boot. As the boot lid lifted, I noticed a large silver case, similar to the cases used by photographers to carry their equipment. As I was asking Mitch what was inside it, John opened the case. He hadn't realised I was standing right behind him and closed it immediately when he heard my gasp of surprise at what was inside. Nestled in the dark-coloured foam was a dismantled rifle with a sight gauge. John told me not to worry, it was just a precautionary measure which would probably be unnecessary but again I was afraid at what I had got everyone into.

After waiting for the OK over the radio from the other police, Mum and I headed down the drive to Adam's house. John and Mitch said they would park up the street in the car, which relieved me because I didn't think Adam's mum and dad could have handled armed police at his birthday party. Everyone was suitably surprised when Mum and I walked in. Adam and I were thrilled to see each other and we spent as much time together as possible. Everyone was asking how Mum and I were doing and what was going on about the threat but we had been told to be circumspect in what we said, so we couldn't tell people much. Mum and I made frequent trips out to the car, taking drinks and cake to John and Mitch. We didn't want them sitting there feeling left out.

The two hours passed far too quickly and before we knew it we were standing by the front door with everyone crowded around. John motioned to us that it was time to leave and with hugs all round, Mum and I walked back to the police, tears pouring down my cheeks. I didn't know when I would see them all again and I knew Mum and I were headed back to obscurity.

When we got back to the apartment, I made everyone a coffee and thanked John and Mitch so much for allowing me to go to the party and told them I understood the amount of work it had meant for them. John said the look on my face and the smile I had carried since arriving at Adam's made it well worth all the effort. Later as we sat alone, Mum and I talked about how good it felt just to have had that small amount of freedom. Like most things, you don't appreciate it until it is snatched away. We felt we had had the same experience as a prisoner on day release. That night I was able to sleep more soundly. As I drifted off to sleep, I made sure my last thoughts were of the party and not of Fred Many. I wanted my last thought to be of happier times and not to give another restless, sleepless night away to Many.

Then two days later we were hit again with the full impact of the situation we were in when we were confronted with a new danger.

John said he had been contacted by the internal investigations department of the police and asked to take us into their offices. His conversation was very short and direct, which we found to be very strange coming from John. We asked him what it was all about but he said that even he didn't know what was going on, it was all extremely official. At the offices, we found the two detectives who had gone to Queensland with Mum waiting for us and as we sat down, we were shocked to hear them asking John to leave the room. Mum and I looked at each other, not knowing what on earth was going on.

They explained they were investigating the possibility that it was indeed a police officer who had leaked Mum's personal details to Many. They believed it was highly likely the officer was from Gosford but they were investigating all the officers we had come into contact with—even our witness protection minders. I refused to believe they could suspect John and

Mitch of any wrongdoing, especially since we were told they were among the elite branch of the police force. However the two detectives wanted to know everything we knew about John and Mitch and all the other officers we had come into contact with. Mum and I felt fragile and threatened all over again. We didn't know who to trust anymore. We were confused, angry and frustrated that this was happening now. As we answered their interminable questions, which I knew were for the best, I thought how bizarre this all was. There I had been, thinking that once I reported the attack to the police they would arrest the man and that would be the end of it. But here we were, not even drawing close to the trial, our freedom snatched away and now we were being told not to trust the very people we had been instructed to trust.

We were eventually reunited with John and he drove us back to the apartment in silence. The detectives had asked us not to discuss the interview with our minders and we felt very guilty having to explain this to John when he asked.

For our safety, we weren't able to stay in the apartment for much longer and over the next few months we were moved many times to different safehouses which I can't discuss for security reasons. John and Mitch could see we were starting to deteriorate pretty quickly. Our sense of humour had left us by this stage. Our nerves were beginning to get quite ragged and our tempers had become quite short. There were no more questions to be asked. All we could do was sit and wait. The days were becoming very long and so were the nights. We had both become quite unbearable. While Mum and I tried so hard to keep calm and rise above all the drama, at times our efforts seemed useless. We tried to keep ourselves amused but you can only read so much or watch so much television. We never even got those jumpers knitted with the wool Mum bought at the start of witness protection. While we had nothing much else to do, we couldn't relax enough to concentrate on the stitches.

The guys continued to be wonderful and tried to keep our spirits up by spending a lot of time with us. They took us out to lunch a few times just to get us out and tried to come up with different topics to talk about. Each little outing kept us going for a few more days. We all became quite close and Mum and I didn't regard them as scary policemen anymore. They had become people who had homes and lives of their own. We realised they were just doing their job but they still managed to make us feel important.

It was like being in solitary confinement. We did have each other but there were times when just the sheer frustration of being locked up was very difficult. Fear was replaced by anger that we had to go through this because of Fred Many. It was a ridiculous situation. We were in a gaol, certainly a comfortable gaol but a gaol all the same, with no contact with the outside world. No-one knew where we were and it was as if we had ceased to exist to the rest of the world. In a way it was worse than gaol because there were no visiting days where we could see our family and friends. It was like being in a capsule in outer space. You could listen in on the radio and find out what was happening in the world but you weren't really part of it.

I felt I deserved all this for getting into that car and for putting Mum through this torment. My punishment was—guilt.

The months rolled on and eventually the police felt the threat had diminished enough for us to get back to some kind of a normal life. I still wasn't allowed to go back to Terrigal but the witness protection people did allow Mum and me to move into a rented flat by ourselves. They took us around real estate agents to find somewhere suitable. Mum and I chose a large converted granny flat in the rear of a house in one of Sydney's suburbs. Witness protection approved it because it was set well back from the road and had a narrow driveway that ran along the side of the main house and around the back to the front door of the flat so it would be difficult for anyone to see us entering or leaving the flat from the road.

We were still using our real names but witness protection organised for the lease, telephone and electricity to be put under different names so we could not be traced. They even paid the bond and the first two months' rent for us which allowed Mum and I to use what money we had to try to turn the flat into a comfortable home. The day Mum's furniture arrived back from storage we really felt we had turned a corner. We were like kids in a toyshop, it was like getting everything new again. However the police explained to us that we were still technically part of witness protection—although we felt as if we were 'on leave'—they would be keeping a regular check on us. We had all their numbers so we could get in touch should we see anything suspicious. We were under strict instructions not to tell people too much and still to be very careful about what we did, where we went and to whom we spoke. So much for thinking we were getting back to normal.

The people Mum worked for had been terrific, holding her job open for her, and now she was able to get back there. The witness protection people gave her their permission to work because the radio station was a very secure building, with a security guard out front and a pass key needed to get through the front doors. She had a lift door to door every day to work because the detectives insisted upon driving her for protection. Most of the people who worked at the station were aware of what had happened and aware of the secrecy still needed but to be on the safe side, the detectives spoke personally to her bosses to impress upon them the care that was needed. On her first day, they organised a huge lunch to welcome her back. She was very popular at work and just seeing that light come back into her eyes in that first week back at work was wonderful.

I soon got myself a job as an office junior with a property management company which pleased the police no end because it was right next door to their building. We had some of our old freedom back but the price paid was that we were constantly looking over our shoulders. It had been drilled into us what we should and should not do. Even when booking a cab we never used the same name twice, something we had a lot of fun with as we tried to think up the strangest names possible. Mum and I called each other several times a day to make sure we were each OK. We were never home late and each of us always knew where the other was and who she was with. Even at home we still checked on each other. I was still having nightmares and if I got up during the night to go to the bathroom or to get a drink, I always looked in on Mum as she did with me. We were very conscious of each other's safety and very protective of each other. The witness protection had changed our relationship by bringing us together in a different way. It was no longer mother and daughter. It was two fugitives together and we really needed and depended on each other.

One day Mum got a call at work from the Office of the Director of Public Prosecutions saying that a date had finally been set for the trial. It was to be 28 February 1988, the next year. When she told me I thought, great, one day before her birthday.

With the trial drawing near, so was Christmas, always a big affair in my family. This year Mum and I decided we wanted everyone at our place, as small as it was. So Aunt Billie and Uncle Greg drove down to Sydney and Billie's younger sister and her husband came along as did Granny. As we sat around the table that day for Christmas lunch pulling crackers and wearing the silly paper hats, laughing and joking and all talking at the same time, it was one of the happiest moments of my life. My family was all that mattered to me.

CHAPTER 10

THE TRIAL

The night before the trial was nerve wracking. It was also quite eerie because Mum and I were completely on our own. Our family and friends knew it was due to start the next morning but none of them called. Everything was silent. The silence, however, was good for me because I needed the time to myself. I had received a taste of what I was in for in the witness box at the committal hearing but, since then, Mum and I had heard a lot about the justice system from people we knew were well meaning but who only served to make us very concerned about what was in store for me. We had been told that giving evidence and being cross-examined could be gruelling. Of course, we also had no idea what Fred Many's defence would be. We knew by now he was a devious man—although we still had no idea how devious—and we knew he would be doing everything he could to discredit me and to get himself out of this situation.

Mum thought I should go over my statement to refresh my memory but I read two paragraphs and put it down. I didn't need to read any further. The events of that night were crystal clear in my mind as if it had happened yesterday and I was ready to get into that courtroom and tell the truth. I hadn't always felt so brave but Mum had pulled off quite a coup a few weeks earlier.

Our minders, John and Mitch, had been transferred to other

departments, much to our distress, and another detective called John had taken over our case. We had no cause to worry because he had been briefed totally and knew what was what. Before I met him, he had phoned Mum to introduce himself and arrange a meeting to talk about the trial. At the meeting, Mum told him she wanted me to see the courtroom and meet with the crown prosecutor who would be presenting our case at the trial. Although her suggestion wasn't scoffed at, it was made clear to her that this was not the done thing. Victims were simply witnesses in the trial having no special rights. Like the other witnesses, they were expected to go to court, give their evidence and leave. But the new John had not bargained on my mum. She had had enough of doing everything she was told to do and became quite aggressive with him. I didn't know she could be so strong and defiant. She told him that she felt I had already given the police and the justice system my all, more than a hundred per cent of my strength, courage and resilience. All she was asking for was a little something back. She even told him that if they wouldn't give a little, they wouldn't have a witness as I would not be giving evidence and that, she said, was that. Within hours, the new John had phoned back and said he had made arrangements and everything Mum wanted was going to happen.

The next day at 12.30 p.m., she met me outside the office where I worked. I had felt upset and insecure when I heard John and Mitch would not be with us for support during the trial and this was to be the first time I came face to face with the new John. The moment our eyes met, I knew I was going to be all right. John, as he told me to call him in that first meeting, was slightly taller than Mum and had a stocky build and a gentle nature (with us anyway). There was something about him that I warmed to straight away. He will be embarrassed about me saying this, but I recognised a father figure in him and soon started seeing him in this light. He made me feel as if nothing could ever hurt me again.

He drove us across to the NSW Supreme Court building at Taylor Square in Darlinghurst. I had passed it every day on my way to and from work but hadn't realised this would be where the trial would be held. It is a huge historic building with columns across the front, very imposing and very much what you would expect a courthouse to look like. We were shown into the crown prosecutor's chambers and introduced to our prosecutor, who was Alexander Dalgleish, a Queen's Counsel. He was a kindly gentleman who sat Mum and me down, explaining the sort of questions he would be asking and what the counsel for the defence would be trying to do. He explained the defence would be trying to discredit me as much as possible to put a different light on what had actually happened. He then asked if Mum and John could leave the room so he could have a word with me in private. I was expecting some questions from him but all he did was chat about a few things and try to put me at ease. He asked if there was anything I was particularly worried about to which I answered not at that stage. I appreciated his kindness immensely. I was still only sixteen and a half and I found the whole process of speaking with a man of his stature quite daunting.

Then he led Mum, John and me down to the courtroom. We walked along what seemed like a labryrinth of corridors until we walked out into a small courtyard. On the opposite side was a heavy steel door leading into a wider corridor where Mr Dalgleish pushed through a pair of large, ornate double doors. He stood aside and allowed me to pass. Nothing could have prepared me for the enormous size of the courtroom. Dark timber panelling lined the walls and heavy timber benches were set up in rows. The doors had opened into the public seating area. In front of this was the long timber table which lawyers call the 'bar table' where the prosecutor and the defence lawyers would be sitting. Along the left side of the courtroom was the raised area containing twelve seats for the jury. Opposite the jury's area was another raised area, the dock, where Many would be sitting. John explained the dock led directly down to the holding cells beneath the court so Many wouldn't have to walk anywhere near me.

Directly in front of us was the most important-looking raised area where the judge would be sitting. To the right of the judge's area was the witness stand and John said there was a corridor which ran alongside the outside of this particular courtroom and opened right into the witness box so I wouldn't have to walk through the public part of the court. The only time I would be seen was the moment I stepped into the witness box.

Having seen what I could expect on the first day of the trial, I felt better prepared and I was grateful to John and the prosecutor for going out of their way for me. That evening, John invited Mum and me out to dinner to get to know each other a bit better and we went to a popular Italian restaurant. At first, the conversation was a little stilted as we had said all there was to say about the trial and were down to small talk. However the small talk soon became raucous laughter. John had a fabulous sense of humour and we found we all clicked. I felt a great kinship with John. I felt I could trust this man with my life. By the end of the night, we all knew we would become fast friends.

The trial had been put back a week and was due to start on Monday, 7 March 1988. That morning I woke up with great anticipation. I knew this was it. Fred Many would either go to gaol or be found innocent and get off and I was going to do my best to make sure it was the former. Only that morning did it hit Mum and me how important the next few hours and days were going to be. Mum and I had packed an overnight bag as John said we would have to stay in a safehouse near the courts during the trial. After everything that had happened to us, it seemed a miracle we had got this far and made it through with our lives.

When John arrived, he came into the granny flat alone but said he had someone to introduce us to, his partner Grahame. I saw a head lean through the front doorway. It belonged to a tall, dark-haired blue-eyed man with a wonderful smile. Grahame appeared fairly quiet and stayed in the background for most of that morning but Mum and I soon discovered that was not normally his nature. In truth he was a very funny and uplifting sort of person. As we headed out to the waiting car, we had no idea when we would be returning to our own little place of safety—our home.

When Mum and I got into the back seat of the car, we noticed there were no door handles. They had been removed and covered over with fittings that matched the interior trim of the car. Grahame had to help me close the door because it was too heavy for me to move it myself. It was a fairly warm morn-ing and we wanted to wind the windows down but the window handles were also missing. John and Grahame explained it was a bulletproofed car. The panels and doors were heavily armoured which was why the door felt so heavy and why the windows could not be opened. As we drove off, it was obvious the car was more difficult than the average car for Grahame to manoeuvre. Grahame said the car was so heavy that the suspension had to be replaced regularly. John explained that this was the day any last ditch attempt would be made on my life to stop me from appearing in court and they needed to take every precaution possible. Not only were they worried about the murder contract but they knew Many was in a circle of violent criminals who they thought wouldn't hesitate to help him.

They drove to the courthouse in the manner Mum and I had become accustomed to—running red lights, going along one-way streets and doubling back. It surprised me how driving as if we were in a Hollywood cop movie no longer fazed me as it had in the early days. I now thought nothing of it and the realisation scared me because it demonstrated how easy it was to become used to this covert business and accept it as a way of life.

As we neared Darlinghurst, John picked up a hand-held radio from out of the central armrest and began to communicate with the officers he said were waiting at the courthouse. He gave a step by step description of where we were located, detailing the cross streets we had reached and constantly updating our estimated time of arrival. As usual, Mum and I wanted to know everything that was happening and John said if anything happened, he wanted the waiting police to know our exact location. He saw the looks of panic cross our faces and reassured us we would be fine.

We rounded a corner and pulled up in front of two huge metal doors. They were large enough to get a car through but looked thick enough to stop a tank. John spoke into his two-way radio and the doors opened slowly. Inside the first gate two armed police officers were standing alert. Grahame drove very slowly along an alley so narrow that we would not have been able to open the car doors fully to get out. There were two more heavy metal doors to go through and at each one, John had to verify who he was and who he had in the car. They were certainly taking no chances. We finally stopped in an area with a bit more space. Almost immediately the car was completely surrounded by more armed police. The back doors of the car were opened and we were hustled out and set off at what was almost a running pace into the courthouse, with John and Grahame following closely behind us. I soon lost all sense of direction as we hurried along the maze of corridors. I felt very uneasy until I recognised the area we had been shown by the crown prosecutor. We were led into a small room. Everywhere I looked there were armed police. They were lined up along the corridor and just before the door to the room was closed behind us, I saw another police officer position himself directly in front of the door. Two more officers stood inside the room. The room was fairly small and getting quite crowded with Mum and me, John and Grahame plus two armed police officers. The room was fairly light and airy, with a table that ran along one wall with tea, coffee and a bowl of biscuits on it. Mum and I looked at each other and knew this was it—the police could only take us so far, now it was up to us to take over and fight for ourselves.

While all the precautions were meant to make us feel safe, they completely unnerved us. Mum and I were still trying to catch our breath when the crown prosecutor arrived. Mr Dalgleish asked the armed police to leave so we could talk in private. He explained what would be happening in the courtroom, about 45 metres along the corridor, they were about to start selecting the jury and once this was done the jurors would be sworn in. Many would be asked to enter a plea to the charges. He was charged with intent to murder, detain with intent to rape, assault and four counts of rape of a person under the age of sixteen. Many was expected to plead not guilty. Mr Dalgleish said that as a victim of a sexual assault, the media would be unable to identify me but just to make sure, the judge, Justice Kenneth Carruthers, would order that my name not be revealed. Then Mr Dalgleish would begin presenting his case and I would be called to give evidence. With that said, he left us to return to the courtroom. Mum and I went back to waiting. We had itchy feet, feeling the time slowly tick by. I got up to walk around but, confined to the small room, I was walking in circles. Mum felt helpless. She tried to talk me through any problems I might have. If I faltered or didn't understand a question, I had to ask them to repeat it; I had to take my time and not rush into my answers; I should take a sip of water and think about the answer; these were Mum's words of advice. I knew it would come down to me against Fred Many in the courtroom.

After what seemed like an eternity, there was a knock on the door. John and Grahame sprang to attention and asked us to get over to the far wall of the room so when the door opened we would not be visible to whoever was there. John checked who was at the door before opening it a little, and then a little more when he felt it was safe to do so. It was a uniformed court officer I had never seen before who told us the court was ready. My deep intake of breath was audible in the room and Mum squeezed my hand tightly. I wished I could have had all that time sitting there waiting and doing nothing all over again.

I made a move towards the door but John shook his head and said the court needed to have Mum testify first. We thought we had everything organised but neither of us had expected this. It was explained that Mum had to give evidence of my date of birth to prove I was a minor at the time of the attack. Mum steadied herself and was soon on her way out the door. We had held each other close and seeing her leave that room to face the unknown just about killed me.

I sat down next to Grahame, put my head in my hands and cried. Not a word was spoken between us, the only way of knowing there was anyone in the room with me was the feel of Grahame's arm around my shoulders, tightening with each sob. I looked at this stranger who was there risking his own life for mine and I asked him why this was happening. Grahame never answered. It was a question without an answer.

Time passed so slowly during Mum's absence. I felt she had been in the courtroom for hours. The longer it took, the angrier I became. I asked myself what they were putting her through in there. The protective feelings

I had for Mum had continued to grow and although I was her daughter, it was me who felt like a lioness protecting her cub. After what seemed like hours but was only about thirty minutes, Mum was led back into the room.

She did not have time to tell me then, but she had been asked just five short questions by the prosecutor: her name, where she lived, her relationship to me, which hospital I had been born in and whether I was outside the court ready to give evidence. Many's barrister, David Elliott, only had a couple of questions in the cross-examination.

When Mum walked back into the room, I pounced on her. But before I could ask if she was OK, she held me by the shoulders and said they were ready for me. I took a deep breath and held on to Mum for as long as I could before the court officer who had led Mum back said it was time for me to go. Mum was about to follow me out when the officer said she had to stay in the room and wait. We both stopped dead in our tracks.

'What do you mean I can't go with her?' asked Mum.

The officer explained I had to give evidence to the court on my own. There just aren't words to describe what Mum and I felt at that time.

With no time to come to terms with the fact I wouldn't be able to see Mum's face while on the witness stand, I was on my way to the courtroom. I was flanked by three armed police officers and when we walked into the small courtyard between our room and the court, I saw another seven officers surrounding the perimeter of the yard. I recognised some of them from our dealings with the witness protection team as being with the Special Weapons and Operations Squad. Some of the men nodded to me as if trying to give me their support. All I could manage was a stiff smile of thanks in response.

One of the officers quietly knocked on the door that led to the corridor outside the court and explained that the police on the other side of the door were making sure the area I had to pass through was clear of people. After a few moments, the door opened and I was led into the corridor that would take me along to the door which opened next to the witness box. I was handed over to another SWOS officer whom I recognised and knew was also called Graeme. He gave me a wink and, placing his hand in the middle of my back, led me along the corridor to yet another SWOS officer whom I had not met before. He was introduced by Graeme as Andrew. Andrew, I was soon to discover, was to be my lifeline.

As Graeme headed back to his post at the end of the corridor, Andrew and I stood and looked at each other. I had to tilt my head to look at him as he was so tall. I knew that once through the door next to us, I would be stepping straight into the witness box. I brought my hand up to my face and it must have been evident I was shaking with fear. Andrew reached for my hand and, holding it gently, brought it away from my face, saying that he wanted to see my smile. He said he had heard all about it. This indeed made me smile and I can remember him saying: 'Wow, what a knockout.' I couldn't believe I was able to smile at a time like that but seeing a friendly face before having to go through what I knew was facing me made all the difference.

Andrew said once I was in the witness box, he could either close the door or leave it open—that way, I would only have to look slightly to my right and he would be right there. I knew if the door was left open he would be able to hear all the evidence, but I needed to see a friendly face. I asked him if he would leave the door open. He very quietly said: 'I'll be right here with you.'

With that, I turned and took the step up to the witness stand.

Straight away, I looked to my right and saw Andrew there. He smiled and made a motion with his hands as if to say: 'See, I'm right here.' I turned to the court. Raising my head in that courtroom was one of the hardest things I have ever had to do.

The first thing I saw was the public gallery opposite me and then the jury to my right. It was a sea of faces, faces of people who by the end of my time in the witness box would know every single detail of what happened that night. The humiliation of it all was almost too much. Then my eyes scanned towards the left of the room where I saw Mr Dalgleish at the centre table and, next to him, the defence lawyers. I faltered there knowing that if I looked any further to the left, I would come face to face with Many, opposite the jury. I tried to force myself to look at him but I just wasn't ready to do that yet. My thoughts were interrupted by the court officer who had approached and was standing in front of me. He had me take the Bible in my right hand. When I tried to speak, nothing came out. I had to clear my throat before I could swear to tell the whole truth and nothing but the truth.

The crown prosecutor rose from his seat.

'Please tell the court your full name?'

'Kirstyn Jean Anna Austin.'

I had sworn to tell the truth and as Mr Dalgleish took me step by step through the events of 2 September 1986, I did exactly that.

He made me start on the morning of 2 September and I told him how I had been to see Susie at Terrigal. I told him about our visit to the chemist where I bought the false nails. I was conscious of the silence in the courtroom as I spoke but I hadn't realised I was speaking so quietly myself until Justice Carruthers interrupted.

'Can the members of the jury hear the witness?' he asked.

The foreman of the jury replied they couldn't hear everything I said, the judge turned to me.

'Just try to keep your voice up,' he said. I nodded and the court officer came towards me with a glass of water. After taking a sip, I continued with my evidence. I did my best to speak up in a clear voice and just kept my eyes fixed on the back wall of the courtroom. I told the court how I went to Wamberal Beach with my friends and left them there as I walked alone towards The Entrance Road. The prosecutor kept asking me what happened next, what happened next. I said a white car pulled up and the driver asked where I was going. I must have still been talking too quietly in my nervousness because Mr Dalgleish asked me to keep my head up.

'When you put it down, I think you get a little bit difficult to hear,' he said. 'What happened next?'

I told him about the conversation I had with the man in the car and how I had eventually got into the passenger seat and we drove off up the hill towards The Entrance. Bit by bit, Mr Dalgleish had me tell the jury about my ordeal. The next part of my evidence was very difficult to speak about in front of so many people, including Many.

'There was a bus stop on the left-hand side and I said to him, "Oh just here would be great, thank you." He kept driving and I said "Can I get out here, please?" He turned around and slapped me across the face,' I said.

Mr Dalgleish wanted me to expand on what had happened.

'He turned around and backhanded me across the face,' I said.

Mr Dalgleish asked me how that felt.

'It hurt,' I said.

As I continued, the prosecutor kept asking me to give more detail about certain events. I had been trying to briefly describe the sexual assaults but the jury needed to hear exact detail. I found this nearly impossible to do. I kept thinking to myself: 'How could they make me repeat all this in front of Many?' Why couldn't they have him leave the courtroom while I am here? I could feel his eyes burning into me as I described the things he did to me. I knew as I went through the details of what he did to me, he would be picturing them in his mind. I felt I was only reminding him, blow by blow, of that day. I felt as if I was going to pass out at any moment. The court officer, who was a lovely, short, older man with a kind face, kept appearing to my left with glasses of water and tissues. It was a human touch which made me feel less isolated.

I had to tell the jury what happened on the journey in the car and how the driver made me have oral sex in the driveway. I told the jury as much as I could remember about the driver and the car, about the cane holder that had the cigarette packet in it, how I had hidden my false fingernails in the brake lights. I answered Mr Dalgleish's questions and it seemed to me that it was all done in such a matter of fact way, almost clinical. I was far too nervous to look at the jury but I told them how the driver took me into a clearing off the Pacific Highway. When I got to the bit where he told me to take off my clothes and then pushed me down on the seat, my voice faltered a bit but I took another sip of water and went on. I knew how important this was. I said he pushed me down and told me to open my legs. Then he pulled his shorts and pants down and had sex with me.

Mr Dalgleish said: 'Pardon.'

'He had sex with me,' I said.

'I'm sorry,' said Mr Dalgleish. 'When you say "he had sex with me", you have got to describe what occurred. What did he do?'

I knew the court needed to hear the exact detail but I felt it was just too personal. Here I was at a rape trial and I was worried about the need for privacy but this was not just about Many, it was about me and I felt all my personal privacy had been stripped from me. No-one warns you of that nor of the fact that the moment you enter this situation you have no rights. You are there to tell the world about the hurtful, soul-wrenching events that have taken your innocence away and everyone is there to hear all the details without a second thought about what it may be doing to you. It is the most embarrassing situation anyone can ever go through.

I looked to my right and saw Andrew at the door. He gave me a reassuring smile and mouthed the words: 'I'm right here.' Knowing I had someone so close helped me but I was also feeling totally ashamed about the fact Andrew would be hearing all those details. No matter how many times I have had to explain the events of that day and night, it doesn't get any easier and the embarrassment never goes away. I just barely managed to get the words out: 'He put his penis in my vagina.' It may sound strange but I felt like a naughty little schoolgirl speaking about a taboo subject.

Mr Dalgleish asked me what happened next. I told him how the man had tried to strangle me and how I had pretended to be dead. I explained to him my time spent in the bush and flagging down the truck driver. I was starting to feel physically exhausted but I didn't want to take a break because I didn't think I would have the strength to go back into the courtroom. The court officer was taking care of me with a steady stream of tissues and refilling my water glass. The tissues ended up in a shredded mess in my lap as I ripped them up to help me through the fear I felt.

Then came the time I had been dreading. As Mr Dalgleish had explained to me in our previous meeting I had to formally identify Many in the court-room. I had been purposely looking away from him although I could feel his eyes on me at all times. I had felt invaded by him all over again. Mr Dalgleish asked me if I had seen the man again at any stage. I explained that before the committal hearing in Gosford I had seen him on the evening news and then again at the committal.

'Have you seen him since that time?' asked Mr Dalgleish.

'No,' I said.

'Is he in the courtroom today?' asked Mr Dalgleish.

'Yes, he is,' I said.

'Whereabouts?' Mr Dalgleish wanted to know.

I said he was over there and I raised my head and looked over to my left, taking in everyone in the courtroom as my eyes moved to where I knew Many was sitting. It felt like I was travelling in a time warp, everything happened so slowly. My eyes took in the glint of the polished wood panels as they shone with the reflection from the overhanging lights; they moved across to the bar table in the middle of the room filled with papers; past the crown prosecutor who was standing expectantly; across to the court officer who had a look of apprehension on his face and finally up to the dock where Many stood. I looked at his torso first, not wanting to look any further, knowing that I had to identify him properly. I raised my eyes to meet his. His eyes were looking straight back at me. They were the cold hard eyes that were so threatening. They were the eyes that I knew, I had seen that day in September. They were the eyes of my rapist. At that point I totally under-stand the phrase about someone's eyes burning into you. That was what I was experiencing. His eyes held no shame, only hatred. I lifted my right arm, pointing directly at Many and told the court that he was the man who raped me.

Mr Dalgleish asked me if I knew him or knew of him or had heard of Frederick Many before that day.

'Of course I hadn't,' I told him.

Then Mr Dalgleish asked the court officer to show me eight

photographs. They were the same photographs I had seen during the committal hearing. They were the ones the police photographer had taken of me on the day of the attack, showing the injuries to my body. Looking at the photographs of myself covered in scratches and gouges and with the bruising around my neck brought back so much pain. The scars on my arms and hands had faded a little but the scars on my legs were still noticeable and something I had to see every day. The scars were a constant reminder of what had happened. I was asked to identify myself in them and confirm that, yes, those were my injuries. Then I was shown more photographs, this time of the clearing. I was pleased the jury was able to see those because I wanted them to see how desolate that clearing was. The last photograph was of the back of a white Galant. I had no doubt it was the very car Many drove that day and I said so.

The crown prosecutor said there were no more questions. I now had to prepare myself for the questions from Many's defence but the judge said I could have a rest and he would adjourn the court for the lunchbreak. He turned to me and said I could step down. I felt so tired and drawn. I rose quietly and stepped out to my right and straight into the arms of Andrew in the corridor. He gave me a huge hug and spoke kindly to me, telling me how well I had done and how I had nailed Many to the wall. I was trembling and I felt very much like a little girl. I needed a father's comforting arms, making do with the arms of a policeman.

Andrew placed an arm around my shoulders and led me back along the corridor where Mum was waiting for me with John and Grahame outside the waiting room. As Mum held me tightly, I felt myself relax in the belief that the worst part was over. Locked up again for our safety in the little room, I told Mum what had happened as we ate the sandwiches the police had brought in. The lunchbreak seemed to take forever and I was starting to get angry again at Many for putting us through this. After letting me talk, John and Grahame started to joke about things they knew would make us laugh to try to lighten things up. They were wonderful to us. Our spirits had started to lift when there was a knock at the door. It was one of the officers bringing a message across from the court. One of the female jurors had become very upset because of the nature of the case and because of the details of my evidence and had asked to be excused from the rest of the trial. I didn't understand what the problem was, assuming the trial would simply continue with eleven jurors. I was wrong. The officer explained that while that would be possible, the decision about whether to continue or empanel a whole new jury had to be made by the defence lawyers, and they were still making up their minds. After a stunned silence from the room, Mum was the first to speak.

'Kirstyn can't go through with that again, she just can't,' she said. She announced I had done my bit, that we were going home right now, stood up and started looking for her handbag before breaking down in tears. I was shellshocked at the prospect of having to go through my evidence again. John said we should stay positive and the judge may decide to go on with this jury. Our hopes were soon dashed when the court officer returned and said the defence had asked for a new jury because they felt that the remaining eleven jurors may have been influenced by the feelings of the juror who could not go on. Mum wondered if my evidence could just be read out to the new jury but the officer explained the judge had ruled that I had to reappear and give the evidence all over again.

I felt so powerless. When I saw how upset Mum was I felt guilty all over again for doing this to her. If I had listened to her advice I would never have got into that car. It would have made things easier if she had been angry with me. But I wasn't going to let Fred Many get away with it and I knew Mum felt the same way. She was just trying to protect me.

'Mum, this is happening. I'm strong enough to go on. Please, let me do this,' I said to her. Of course I did not need her permission but this calmed her down. We were really functioning as one person by this time—I hardly needed to say anything, she knew what I was thinking.

I felt I needed some space and asked Grahame if it was safe for me to step outside. He checked and saw the courtyard was still surrounded by SWOS officers. He allowed me to go out there with him to get a breath of fresh air.

The sun was streaming in, filling the yard. Standing there feeling the warmth on my skin and taking lungfuls of air made me feel a little more at ease. I saw that in the wall around the perimeter of the yard were small low-set windows. At the same time, Grahame noticed that one of these windows was open and quickly ushered me back into the corridor outside the waiting room, explaining that the windows opened into the holding cells beneath the court and he didn't want to take any chances that Many was in the cell with the open window, although it was so small no-one could fit through it.

I didn't want to go back inside that little room and saw another door further along the corridor which Grahame had earlier said led to the court library. With their permission, I let myself in. It was a big room and its walls were lined with shelves and shelves of books. I was engulfed by that rich musty smell of old leather you sometimes notice in antique shops. I moved to close the door but Grahame asked me to leave it open. In the middle of the library was a long narrow wooden bench used to lean the books on. I rested my hip against the bench and tried to read, or rather to understand, the titles on the legal books. I thought about how everyone was relying on me to see this through. There were all the officers who had been involved throughout the case and the police who were standing outside to protect me. Then there was Mum and all this was doing to her. One moment I was standing there in that strange room, the next I was falling to the floor. Once I was aware I was falling, everything blacked out. I must have landed with quite a thud because Grahame was in the room in a flash. I felt myself hit the floor and seemed to regain some control again and I was heaving myself up by the bench when Grahame reached me.

I tried to brush it off as if nothing had happened but Grahame saw through that and gave me a look that said: 'I'm not an idiot, Kirstyn.' My hands were shaking. Grahame said I was as white as a ghost. I begged him not to say anything to Mum and he nodded his head. He got me a glass of water and I assured him I was feeling much better. The colour soon returned to my face and Grahame and I rejoined Mum. I kept trying to convince her

I could handle the prospect of going back through my evidence in court and after a while, I even started to believe it myself.

After another interminable wait, the court officer came to tell us that the rest of the afternoon would be taken up with swearing in the new jury and that we could leave and start afresh in the morning. Although it was putting off the inevitable, I felt so much better at the thought of not having to go back in the witness box until the next day.

We retraced our steps along the corridors to reach the armoured car and drove to an apartment block in the city. Once we had settled in, I asked if I could take a walk and was surprised when John agreed. He accompanied me but as we walked the streets, he kept his hand on my elbow at all times. I joked that I had no plans to skip town but John was being very protective and kept his firm grip on me.

When we got back to the apartment, I was pleased to see Mum smiling. She and Grahame were having a giggle about something and over dinner that night, we felt we were able to unwind a little. We got word from the prosecutor that the judge had said Mum could sit in the court when I gave my evidence again, which was a huge relief. But the night passed very slowly and I got little sleep. My mind was racing. I was worried that somehow I might say something different to the evidence I had just given but I reminded myself that everything I had said was the truth so I need not worry about making mistakes. As I lay awake, I tried to work out what Many's defence would be—but I had no idea how far he would go.

CHAPTER 11

THE LIES

'I want to suggest to you that in the last week of August 1986 you met Mr Many outside the pink hotel, the Union Hotel, in Gosford.'

It did not take long for Many's barrister, David Elliott, to get to the heart of Many's defence as he cross-examined me when we were all back in court the next day with a new jury. I said that, of course, I had never met Many before 2 September, the day of the attack, but then Mr Elliott suggested I had in fact met him not once but several times, including both the Saturday and Sunday of the weekend before the attack. I looked at Mr Elliott as he stood there opposite me at the bar table and I could tell I was going to cry. I had figured out what Many's defence was—he was trying to make out that I had been his girlfriend. The barrister asked if I would like a moment to collect myself but I just wanted to keep going and get this over with.

'No,' I said.

When I had walked into the witness box that morning I had thought it was going to be easier for me because I knew what to expect. I hadn't expected this. Andrew, with his look of encouragement, was there again in the corridor just outside where I was sitting and I could see Mum sitting in the public seats a few rows from the back with John and Grahame. While they all gave me a new sense of security, I felt embarrassed all over again when going through the details of what had happened. John and Grahame had been told the bare facts of the case and I could see the shocked looks on the faces as they heard the full story.

I could see John and Grahame were pressed up against either side of Mum and judging by the look on her face, I could guess why. Her eyes were glued to Many in the dock and I later found out that she was physically shaking with anger. John and Grahame were each holding one of her hands and whispering to her to look at me. I knew Mum would never do anything like shout something out or try to injure Many in any way but she certainly looked as if that was exactly what she wanted to do.

As Mr Dalgleish took me through the same evidence I had given the previous day, I became more and more upset in the witness box. It was a reaction I had not had the day before but having Mum, John and Grahame in the courtroom must have made me feel more relaxed to the point where I allowed my emotions to show. The crown prosecutor asked his final question and as he sat down, the friendly face of the court officer appeared before me offering me a glass of water and yet another tissue. The judge wanted to know if I needed a break before being cross-examined and I said I wanted to go on. I looked over at Mum, who mouthed the words: 'Are you sure?' I gave her the tiniest nod and she gave me the most beautiful encouraging smile. She told me later that she thought I looked very fragile in the witness box because I was slim and I looked so young— although I felt I had been through so much I couldn't possibly be that young anymore.

Then Mr Elliott rose from his seat and turned to face me. He started by asking me what I thought were a few strange, if seemingly innocuous, questions. He jumped from one topic to another and I was confused about what he was doing. The questions ranged from whether I bit my nails to whether Dad had been building a house at Terrigal. He asked me a horrible question about whether the man who attacked me was circumcised or not. I couldn't remember and I told him so. I didn't want to remember it either. Then he moved to the idea of Many and me having an affair, suggesting that I had been using the name Sarah during our 'relationship'. I answered no before he could finish the question. He seemed to change tack for another six or seven questions before asking if I knew a woman whose first name was Robyn. I had no idea who she was. Nor at the time did I know the other names he asked me about—Lyndie or a woman called Patricia. He moved back to this 'affair', a story which Many had been working hard on. Mr Elliott went on to suggest I had been meeting Many at pre-arranged times and places and asked me specifically about a meeting I supposedly had with him on the last weekend of August at the Union Hotel. He suggested that as I waited for Many, I had a conversation with a man who came out of the hotel and asked me if I wanted to join him for a drink. Of course my answer was once again no. I looked at the defence lawyer in a way that said: 'Are you crazy?' I could feel myself getting more and more upset at his questions. 'How dare you ask these things!' I thought to myself. I could not believe he could suggest something so hurtful and also appear to believe it. No-one had warned me that defence barristers are good actors. I now understand that he was just doing his job and that other barristers may have been more brutal with me, but it makes it no easier to understand.

He asked me about whether the man in the car that day had any difficulty hearing me. I hadn't noticed that he had a hearing problem and said so. It was not until much later that I learned Many was partially deaf in one ear, for which he later wore a hearing aid. He had thought he had succeeded in killing me after his first attempt that night in the bush because his deafness meant he could not hear my shallow breathing.

After a few questions, Mr Elliott said he had nothing more and sat down. I was free to go. I walked out of the door into the corridor with such a sense of relief. Mum left at the same time from another exit. John and Grahame were keen for us to move out of the main building and back into our safe little room so with John behind us and Grahame in front, we were ushered along the corridor. We looked like a convoy walking through the waiting area. It was then that Mum and I received a reality check.

Along the left-hand wall of the main waiting area was a row of seats stretching into the corridor. At the far end sat a scruffy-looking man with his legs stretched out in front of him. As we approached, he placed his feet up against the wall of the corridor to block our path in a menacing way. John strode up to him and, without stopping, kicked his legs out of the way. The rest of the waiting area was empty and the sound echoed. It sounded violent. When we got outside, John explained the man had been waiting to give evidence on behalf of Many. Chills went through me at the thought of being so close to someone who was trying to help Many get away with what he had done. John and Grahame asked if I wanted to go back into court and listen to the rest of the trial, which I had the right to do, but I just wanted to get away from there.

After collecting our things from the little room, John and Grahame whisked us back to the secret apartment. The relief Mum and I felt was infectious and we were all soon laughing at silly jokes. I felt I had done my best in court. I said I didn't care what happened from then on—even though I really did care, there just wasn't anything I could do about it. It was up to the crown prosecutor, the judge and jury. When exhaustion finally set in, I had a hot shower and managed to get some much needed sleep.

The next day, Mum and I thought we were going to be confined in our latest prison, this apartment, but John and Grahame had other plans. They arranged to pick us up later in the morning but wouldn't tell us what surprise they said they had planned. It turned out to be a trip on the police boat around Sydney Harbour. As we rode around the water on what was a beautiful sunny day, John told the two of us over and over how well he thought we were doing. It meant a lot to Mum and me that John and Grahame were able to recognise just how difficult the trial was and how hard it was being in witness protection. Some of the police involved in witness protection had spent so much time dealing with criminals, who were usually the ones under witness protection, that they seemed to have become hardened to the victims of crime. I felt lost among the villains in life and not separated from them.

•　•　•

I had no idea what was happening in court. I knew Many had witnesses to testify for him and I realised he would be trying to prove I was lying. I found myself wondering what sort of person would stand in a court of law and try to help someone who could do what Many had done. For the next couple of days, Mum and I just sat in the apartment waiting for news of the trial ending. Since then, I have gone through the transcript because as things developed over the next few years, I wanted to know everything I could about Fred Many.

I learned later that the truck driver who had saved me that morning had to give evidence about finding me by the side of the road. Now I wish I had known he was at court so I could have thanked him again for what he did. Some of the police officers had to give evidence, including Brian Collis, as head of the investigation. A friend of Many's from Gosford, Peter, also gave evidence for the prosecution. Peter's testimony was important because he described the cigarette case and lighter case Many owned—and it was exactly as I had described them to police. Surprisingly, they hadn't been made of cane as I had thought but out of matches which had been varnished to look like cane.

Mum and I hadn't expected Many to go into the witness box and give evidence. He had the right to say nothing or to give an unsworn statement from the dock in which he could say anything and not be questioned on it, a practice which has since been banned in New South Wales. We weren't surprised that he chose to give evidence. He was arrogant and probably thought he could pull the wool over the jury's eyes. He also had nothing to lose. If he was convicted, he was going to go to gaol for a very long time.

Many began his evidence by swearing to tell the truth, which was a bit of a farce. Reading through the transcript was also the first time I got to know who 'Robyn' I had been asked about was. It became obvious that the 'Lyndie' his barrister had asked me about had been his wife, Lyndie Cashman.

Many claimed he had telephoned Robyn, who lived in Sydney, on 1 September, the day before the attack, to wish her a happy birthday and invited her up to the Central Coast the following day. He said she had brought her friend, Patricia, with her. He had met them at Saratoga shopping centre because he didn't want them to go to his house because his mother-in-law, whom he was then living with, would have told his wife.

'I wanted to see her because we were having an affair, me and her, and I didn't want it to go on any longer because we thought my wife was having a baby and we found out later that she was having a baby and I wanted to meet Robyn and tell her that I just thought we should end our relationship the way it was,' said Many.

His story was that they had driven in Robyn's car to the Bay Village shopping centre at Bateau Bay where Lyndie worked in the K-mart store. Many claimed Lyndie's car, the white Galant, had broken down that morning in the Bay Village car park and he had gone to fix it. He said he collected the keys from Lyndie in the store. He said he sat with Robyn and Patricia in Robyn's car and talked till 5.30 p.m. which was when Lyndie finished work at which time Robyn had to leave otherwise they would have been caught together. With that convoluted story, Many thought he had done two things—given himself an alibi in Robyn and Patricia and also explained he couldn't have picked me up in the car because it had broken down and had been in the car park all day.

Then Many moved on to the Union Hotel. He said he had met a man there on several occasions including, significantly, the time, in late August 1986, I had been questioned about in cross-examination. He said he only knew the man as BJ and had gone to the hotel 'to pick up Sarah, Kirstyn Austin'.

He claimed our relationship began after he met me one afternoon in late July in the car park at Bay Village while he had been waiting for his wife to finish work. Many claimed he had seen me on the Saturday and the Sunday of the weekend before the attack but, of course, denied he had attacked me on the Tuesday. As I read the transcript I could picture him sitting there in the witness box. He had obviously spent a lot of time making up his story because he seemed to have an answer for everything. He said he didn't have the cigarette case made out of matches with him on 2 September because he had mistakenly left it in Robyn's car on the Friday before. But how, I wondered, was he going to explain my fingerprints and nails in the boot of his wife's car? He claimed that when he saw me on that weekend I had opened the boot of the car to do something but he did not know what.

As I read on, I realised the significance of those weird questions I had been asked. Many claimed 'Sarah' bit her nails and told him her father was building a house in Terrigal. How he knew about the new house I don't know but the police at Gosford would have known that. I wondered if the same person who gave Many Mum's address had also told him about the house. I don't like to think anyone would betray us like that and once again I thought that if it was one of the Gosford police, it was not one of the ones working directly on our case.

Many claimed he hadn't been able to find his wife Lyndie to come and give evidence for him to support his story about the broken-down car. It was another convenient lie because he knew she was sick of lying for him. That was all Many had to say in his evidence and then it was the turn of the crown prosecutor, Mr Dalgleish. He began slowly but surely pinning Many down on the 'details' of our so-called relationship. Many said he met me every day at the Gosford dole office and we'd go for drives. I was able to so accurately describe to police the rug he had in his car because I had taken it out of the boot on both the Saturday and Sunday of that weekend so we could have sex on it—that made me so sick when I read that. But Mr Dalgleish went on to pick at the holes in Many's story, holes which got bigger and bigger as the questioning went on.

First he started on the lie that Lyndie's car had broken down—but she had driven it to work at one o'clock in the afternoon and she had no reason to use it after that, so how would she know it wouldn't start when she wouldn't use it again until 5.30 p.m. when she finished work? Many had no credible answer for that one. Mr Dalgleish then moved on to a statement Many had made not long after his arrest to Detective Sergeant John Davidson, the police officer he had tried to convince that he was innocent.

The prosecutor showed Many the statement and if I was a betting person, I would have bet that Fred Many wished he had never made it. Detective Davidson had given it to the prosecution but Many obviously had no idea the prosecution had their hands on it. It contradicted the story he had just told the jury. Mr Dalgleish read out parts of the document and I would have loved to have seen Many's face as his own words were being used against him.

'The next time I saw Sarah was on 2 September at Saratoga shopping centre. She rang me and told me she wanted to see me. I told her that I couldn't see her that day because I had to see a friend of mine, Robyn, at the Saratoga shops at 2.00 p.m.,' Many had told Detective Davidson.

'At the time it was about a quarter past one. Sarah told me that she was at Saratoga shops so I told her I would see her. I walked down to the shopping centre and Sarah was there at the bus stop. We started talking and she started talking a bit louder. I didn't want everyone to hear what we were talking about so we went to the lookout. We only went about halfway up. We had a talk for a few minutes and then we made love.'

I was riveted as I read this part of the transcript, it revealed so much about Many, about how devious he was and what a cunning liar he was. It showed me how good he was at making up fairytales because he padded them out with little details to give them the semblance of the truth. It was an art he was to perfect over the following years.

Mr Dalgleish: 'You did have sexual intercourse with a girl named Sarah on 2 September. Is that right?'

Many: 'Yes, I did, sir.'

Mr Dalgleish: 'That is completely contrary to what you said earlier here in court, is it not?'

Many: 'I just forget, sir.'

So, Many had tripped himself up badly. To be a good liar you have to have a good memory. Mr Dalgleish put it to him that he was telling a tissue of lies to exonerate himself from the charges he faced. While Many denied that, Mr Dalgleish had not finished with him. Many had told Detective

Davidson in that first statement that he had picked me up on 2 September at the dole office—but he had just told the court he did not have the car because it was broken down outside Bay Village. Mr Dalgleish continued to read from the statement. It continued that after seeing me on 2 September, he had met Robyn at Saratoga shopping centre—but nowhere in the statement was mention made of Robyn's friend, Patricia, supposedly being there. Mr Dalgleish wanted to know how well Many knew Robyn. Many said he had known Robyn for maybe seven years. She was in love with him.

Mr Dalgleish: 'You say out of regard for your wife's pregnancy you were going to cease the association with her?'

Many: 'Yes.'

Mr Dalgleish: 'That was the reason for the visit, is that right?'

Many: 'Yes, it was.'

Mr Dalgleish: 'Out of regard for your wife?'

Many: 'As far as I can remember, yes, sir.'

Mr Dalgleish: 'That was the same day that you took, according to what you told the police officer, Sarah to Saratoga and had sex with her, was it not?'

Many: 'Yes, it was.'

There was no other answer he could give really! He had backed himself into a corner. The judge asked Many a few questions. What was correct, he wanted to know, that Many had seen Sarah on 2 September as in the statement or that he had not, as he had earlier told the court? Many said he had seen Sarah on 2 September, but had forgotten all about it, that was all. With that ringing in the jury's ears, Many left the witness box and walked back to the dock.

I could hardly believe the evidence of the first witness called by Many's defence lawyer. It was a man whose initials spelled BJ—the man Many said he knew from the Union Hotel. BJ claimed that one night in late August he was on his way back from Queensland when he called into the pink hotel for a drink. He claimed he had seen me outside the hotel and even identified me as the girl he had seen earlier in the witness box. He said I told him I was waiting for my boyfriend and that a little white Galant pulled up and I got into it with the driver, Fred Many. Once again, Mr Dalgleish made a meal of the witness. He asked if it could be that he was not telling the truth about seeing me outside the hotel. Then he moved in for the kill. BJ had a string of convictions for dishonesty, and other convictions which Mr Dalgleish ran through one by one for the benefit of the jury. There was break, enter and steal; two counts of driving while disqualified; stating a false name and address to deceive a police officer and the illegal use of a motor vehicle.

Mr Dalgleish: 'Are you going along with the accused here to give him some sort of support?'

BJ: 'No.'

I was surprised that Many had friends who would stick their necks out for him, there was more to come. The next witness called was the woman called Patricia, who said she had driven up from Victoria to spend 1 September with her friend Robyn because it was Robyn's birthday. She echoed Many's story about her and Robyn meeting him at Saratoga shopping centre on 2 September and then going to Bay Village. She said she and Robyn had left around 5.30 p.m. They even waved to Many as they drove away.

Patricia said that some time later, Many had asked her to help find BJ and she had gone to the Union Hotel every night for a week looking for him. I thought this was an incredibly time-consuming favour for a man she had met only once, that day at Saratoga. Mr Dalgleish must have thought so too and quizzed her about it among other points of her story which did not add up.

Fred Many's next witness was Robyn herself. I wished by now that I had been in court so I could have watched her give evidence because I still have never seen her. She said she had met Many in December 1981 and their relationship developed into an affair by August 1986. She said he had rung her at home on 1 September and wished her a happy birthday. He had arranged to see her the next day. Her story of the journey to Saratoga was identical to that told by her boyfriend Many and her friend Patricia. She also backed up his story saying that he had left his cigarette case in her car on the Friday so on 2 September, it was at her house and not in his wife's car. I couldn't wait to read on and see what the prosecutor had in store for Robyn.

'It was not 1 September that you went to see him for your birthday?' he asked.

Robyn: 'No.'

Mr Dalgleish: 'I see, you did say it was 1 September that you saw him initially, did you not?'

Robyn: 'No.'

Mr Dalgleish: 'Did you not make a statement saying you saw him on 1 September?'

Robyn: 'No.'

But he must have been by now waving that very statement in his hand because the transcript showed he had shown it to her. It was a written statement she had made in front of Many's solicitor. She had to agree that in the statement she had said: 'I arranged on Monday, September 1 to meet Fred at Saratoga shopping centre to talk about the fact that his wife was pregnant.' Robyn told the court that what she had meant was that she had arranged with Many on 1 September to meet with him on 2 September but Mr Dalgleish pointed out that that was not what it said in the statement she had made earlier. Then Mr Dalgleish revealed that a few months later, in January 1987, she had made a second statement in which she tried to put right what she had said in the first statement. In the second one, she said it had been on 1 September when she arranged to meet him on 2 September. But she had still tripped herself up.

Under Mr Dalgleish's cross-examination, she agreed that in the second statement, she had been very careful to get all the details correct because she had realised the mistake she had made in the first statement. However he pointed out that in the second statement, she said that it was she who had rung Many to arrange 2 September. In court, she had said it was Many who rang her. Also, nowhere in her first statement did she mention that Patricia was with her at any time on the day she met with Many.

• • •

While all this drama was going on at court, Mum and I were becoming restless back in the apartment. Grahame had been checking regularly to keep us up to date with what stage the trial was at. By Friday, the lawyers were well into their summations of the evidence and the judge was ready to start his address. However the jury had asked if they could go home and return on the Monday to consider their verdict so we still had the weekend to get through.

Mum and I were desperate to return to our home and both John and Grahame agreed it was a good idea. They felt it was safe enough. We spent Friday night at home on the phone, talking about the trial to friends and relatives. A girlfriend of Mum's from the place she worked came over with some wine and stayed until quite late. It was wonderful to speak to someone who wasn't a police officer, a court official or a lawyer. At one point, I caught myself watching Mum laughing and thinking how good it was to see her having fun again. She felt I had been brave to return to the court the second time and go through my evidence again and made a point of telling me that whenever she could. Mum is terrific at making me feel good about myself.

Once Mum's friend had left, she and I curled up on the sofa together and talked about how lovely it was to finally be home, to be alone and to be able to chat openly about the trial. We were concerned not only about whether Many would be convicted but whether he would be convicted of attempted murder as we had been told this was a hard offence to prove. It was important to everyone involved in our case that the jury find him guilty on that charge because it carried a longer sentence than the other charges. Mum and I were also terrified about what would happen to us if Many was acquitted—would he come looking for us himself?

When Sunday night came around, Mum and I found we were so keyed up, we couldn't sleep. I heard her get getting up in the middle of the night and would join her for glasses of milk or water. By the third time we met in the kitchen, we both laughed a little at how nervous we were and finally by five o'clock in the morning we gave up trying to sleep and reached for the coffee.

John and Grahame had arranged to pick us up at nine-thirty that morning to go to court and await the verdict but Mum and I were ready and waiting by eight o'clock. We both spoke of the possibility of a not guilty verdict—we had to prepare ourselves for the worst.

The trip to court that morning was a little more relaxed. The two police officers arrived in John's usual car and not the armoured car. As I had already given my evidence, they did not feel as though I was in as much danger. However the security at court was still tight with armed SWOS officers surrounding the perimeter of the courthouse. By about ten o'clock, the judge had finished what he had to say and the jury had retired to consider its verdict. Mum and I had heard all the horror stories about the length of time, hours and even days, juries can take to reach a verdict. Having become accustomed to expecting the worst, we did just that. We thought we would be waiting in that little room forever. It was unbelievably tense.

Then, to everyone's surprise, just after morning tea, at 11.30 a.m., we were called into the courtroom to hear the jury's decision. Mum and I looked at each other, both thinking: 'Oh my God, has the case been thrown out?' The police tried to reassure us. They said it was a good indication because it meant the jury had not had to discuss the evidence; it was cut and dried; open and shut. They had seen more juries at work than we had. Mum and I held hands very tightly and took a deep breath as we were led back into the courtroom together to await the verdict.

Security was very tight with police all around us and standing at the doors of the courtroom. The public seats were almost full and I saw a lot of faces I knew. Most of the officers who had been involved with the case over the past eighteen months were there, including Bill, John and Grahame's boss from SWOS. The police told us later that some of Many's friends were also there. The only seats left for us were to the right of the courtroom, in the front row—near Fred Many. Mum and I squeezed in next to each other and John and Grahame fitted in behind.

From the corner of my right eye I could see Many. We were sitting so close to him that I could hear the floorboards creak as he shifted his weight. In an effort not to see him, I turned slightly towards Mum, who was sitting on my left. I felt a hand on my shoulder, giving it a little squeeze and knew it was Grahame giving me reassurance.

A door in the left of the court opened and in walked the members of the jury. I tried not to look at them during my evidence but I now felt able to look into the faces of the people who had heard all the details of what had happened to me. The first person to walk through the door was an older man with a kind face. He sat in the front row at the end closest to Mum and me and as he sat down, he looked right at me, winked his eye and gave the tiniest smile. I couldn't believe what I had seen but I knew I wouldn't have been the only one to see it. Mum squeezed my hand and whispered: 'Did you see that?' I squeezed her hand back and nodded my head. I was too nervous to speak. The judge told Many to stand up and then the judge's associate asked the jury if they had reached a verdict. The foreman said that, yes, they had. Then the judge's associate, who sat in front of the judge, read out the first charge, the assault, and asked if they found Many guilty or not guilty. Mum and I took a deep breath and waited for the answer.

'Guilty.'

Mum and I just looked at each other with beaming smiles on our faces. The relief we felt was overwhelming but we knew it wasn't over yet and we had to stay calm until a verdict had been given on each of the six further charges; two counts of sexual intercourse without consent, detaining with intent, two counts of sexual assault—and the attempted murder. As each time the jury foreman said 'Guilty', I felt we were one step closer to everything we had gone through in witness protection being worthwhile. We were pretty subdued in court, we didn't cheer or make any sound, but inside we were bubbling with happiness. The judge thanked the jury and said they were excused but they all stayed on in the court to hear what was going to happen. Brian Collis was called to the witness box and read out Many's previous criminal history, every count, every charge including the armed robberies and the escapes and attempted escapes, and every sentence. Then he told the judge how Mum and I had been in witness protection after the National Crime Authority intercepted the telephone call from gaol. I could see the looks on the faces of the jury. They knew they had made the right decision.

At that point, Mr Elliott's instructing solicitor came over to Mum and me and said Many would be taking the stand and would need to walk directly in front of us. John and Grahame did not like the idea of that and asked some people to move from seats at the back of the court so we could move back there. I was not aware until later that we had ended up sitting behind some of the friends of Many who had testified against me. Again, John and Grahame sat on each side of Mum and me. Grahame's leg was pressed firmly up against mine and he turned towards me, placing his arm across the back of the seat in front of me, shielding me just in case the people in front turned around to do something. Many's evidence was very brief, just four short answers to four short questions. His barrister asked him if he knew anything about the telephone call or the murder contract and Many denied all knowledge or involvement.

Justice Carruthers adjourned for a short time to consider his sentence, giving us a chance to let off steam.

As we left the court, Mum and I were surrounded by the police both from Gosford and from SWOS—we hugged everyone. John and Grahame were anxious to get us away from the court for fear of reprisals from Many's friends. They ushered us out of the door and we arranged to meet everyone at a nearby hotel in Darlinghurst. We were ready to celebrate big time. The relief that it was finally over was immeasurable. We were joined in the hotel by the detectives from Gosford, John and Grahame and some of the SWOS officers, who I suspect were also there to keep an eye on Mum and me. The court officer who had been so nice to me when I was in the witness box also came to have a drink with us. We felt euphoric.

John got a call on his mobile from the court to let us know about the sentence Many had received. Justice Carruthers had gaoled him for a total of twenty years with no non-parole period, which we thought meant he could not get out earlier. He was going to be in gaol until 4 March 2006.

Justice Carruthers was quoted as saying: 'The prisoner has never shown a glimmer of contrition for the awful wrong which he has done to this young woman. To this moment he remains steadfastly unrepentant. His record is appalling and it leaves one with a sense of despair in this sentencing exercise.'

After a few glasses of champagne, Mum went off to the public telephone to ring everyone she knew, even the radio station, and tell them the news. It was such a happy feeling in the hotel. Even Many's barrister, David Elliott, and his solicitor joined us and turned out to be very nice.

After the hotel, John, Grahame, Mum and I went off for a quiet drink together before heading into Chinatown for lunch. At the restaurant, I was surprised but thrilled to see all the SWOS guys were there including Andrew, which gave me a chance to thank him for being so understanding while I gave my evidence. Two huge tables needed to be pushed next to each other to accommodate everyone, about sixteen people, and we all sat down to a banquet lunch. The lunch turned out to be one of the most wonderful memories I have.

After the meal, Andrew stood up and called for everyone's attention. He then asked me to stand up and join him. I hated being the focus of attention and had no idea what was going on. Andrew then made a speech, talked about the courage he said I had shown, presented me with a black SWOS pin and made me an honorary member of the SWOS team. Everyone applauded and I thanked the guys very much. John then stood up and also made a speech before presenting me with a grey SWOS pin, which only the instructors wear. It is an exclusive pin, which only a few people in Australia have, and I have treasured both those pins to this day. It made me quite teary. The kind words, the help and of course the care those people had shown to Mum and me really touched me. I have yet to meet people whom I respect as highly as those people from SWOS. They alone made things more bearable for Mum and me.

After a very, very long lunch, we spent the evening with Grahame and

John. It was a sad time because we knew we would no longer have the same contact with them that we had enjoyed during the past year. When they finally had to leave, it was hard for us to say goodbye to them. They wouldn't let Mum and me use the 'goodbye' word and insisted we just say: 'See you soon.'

Back at our flat, two friends from Mum's work were waiting for us with a huge bouquet of flowers and the party carried on. I went out with some friends and didn't get home until six o'clock in the morning. It was a long night and for the first time in what seemed like ages, one filled with laughter. We knew Fred Many was going to gaol for a long time.

Of course Many still had seven years, two months and seven days left to serve from his previous sentence from which he was released from gaol early for 'saving' the life of the prison governor. Criminals who break parole, which Many did by attacking me, are liable to return to gaol to serve out the whole of the original sentence. In Many's case, the judge revoked the balance of his earlier sentence, which meant he no longer had to serve it. However we felt that a sentence of twenty years with no prospect of release on parole was a pretty hefty sentence and we were satisfied with it.

With Fred Many behind bars for a long time, we finally thought it was all over.

CHAPTER 12

THE GREAT ESCAPE

To Fred Many, his conviction and twenty-year gaol sentence were just a glitch in his plans. He had known there was more than a fair chance he would be found guilty—which was why he had been working on his escape plan ever since he was arrested. He'd escaped from gaol before and made several unsuccessful attempts at it but this time engineering his escape was going to rely more on cunning than on brute force. Instead of guns and violence, he was going to do it all legally.

Between his prison cell and the courts, 1988 turned into a busy year for him. He was being looked after in the protected section of Long Bay Gaol, both because he was a sex offender and because he was a 'dog' who informed on his gaol mates; he had his extra privileges like the telephone calls and he was the only prisoner in the gaol with his own electronic keyboard. As an informer, he spent a fair amount of his time in interviews with the New South Wales Police, the National Crime Authority and with officers with the Internal Investigations Unit of the gaol, interviews which made him feel important. Lyndie Cashman had ditched him but Robyn was sticking faithfully by his side and visiting him regularly.

As for Mum and me, a few days after the trial ended, the full magnitude of everything really hit us. We had been told we were both still officially part of the witness protection scheme but contact with the group was now at a minimum. We knew we had to try to get back to normal but doing it was very difficult. We had become accustomed to all the drama that had surrounded us during the previous eighteen months.

The media had been reporting on the trial and there were times when Mum and I would find ourselves chatting with people on the bus or in a local shop and they would mention the case. We had to be careful not to allow those people to know the stories were about us. The witness protection group had impressed upon us the fact that there was still, to some degree, a danger to us. They feared that now, Many, instead of trying to stop me giving evidence, may be seeking revenge. Living a life of secrecy and having to be suspicious of everyone made Mum and me a little anti-social. There were very few people we could trust.

It took us a long time to stop feeling like fugitives in hiding but slowly we started to feel more comfortable about going out. I was working as a receptionist and loved the freedom I regained. I surrounded myself with new friends and even started to go out at night. This was a huge step for me after over eighteen months of staying at home reading books and watching videos. It had been a lonely life for a teenager. Although Mum and I relished our new freedom, we still phoned each other regularly when either of us was out. My friends couldn't understand why anyone would be calling home as much as four times during a night out. I would make up some story about the house having been broken into or some such tale. I could not afford to let people know about my past.

As I was trying to get my life back on track, I knew nothing at the time about all the deals Many was doing with whoever would listen to him. It seems to me very unfair that with one hand the National Crime Authority was protecting Many and rewarding him with strange gifts like the keyboard, and with the other hand protecting Mum and me by keeping us in witness protection because they believed Many wanted us killed. It was a bizarre state of affairs. But the National Crime Authority couldn't have been too happy when in August 1987, the charge against Tom Domican alleging he had murdered Christopher Flannery had finally made it to a committal hearing in Sydney's Central Local Court—and despite the gift of the electronic keyboard, Many had refused to give evidence. He was the sole crown witness and without his evidence, the prosecution had nothing. On 18 August, the charge was dropped.

Strike one against Many.

In late 1988, a few months after his own trial, Many was back in the witness box of the NSW Supreme Court, this time giving evidence against Domican in the trial involving the attempted murders of Flannery and his family. This was the charge on which Domican had originally been gaoled in October 1986. Since his gaoling, the case against him had been strengthened somewhat—he had once again allegedly confessed all to none other than Fred Many. The charges had been laid by the New South Wales Police and this time Many performed better than he had in the witness box for the National Crime Authority. In September 1988, Domican was convicted and gaoled for fourteen years with a minimum non-parole period set at ten years.

Before long Many was back in the witness box again. In March 1989, thanks mainly to his evidence, Tom Domican and Peter Drummond were convicted in the NSW Supreme Court of the conspiracy to murder Franciscus Vandenburg. Domican was also convicted of soliciting Many to carry out the murder. Domican received a second gaol sentence of fourteen years, with a non-parole period of ten years. Drummond was gaoled for fourteen years and his non-parole period set at eight years.

Then in March 1990 came the first hint that things were not going all Fred Many's way. The NSW Court of Criminal Appeal overturned the convictions of Domican and Drummond for the Vandenburg conspiracy and ordered new trials—after hearing evidence that Many had lied at the trial. It is rare for the Appeal Court to hear fresh evidence but in this case they made an exception after one of Sydney's best-known criminal solicitors, Leigh Johnson, had come forward. She told the court that Many had approached her while she had been visiting clients in the Special Protection Unit at Long Bay Gaol in April 1989. It had been barely a month after the end of the

Vandenburg trial. Tall, slim, blonde and a good listener, Johnson was popular with prisoners. Glancing around nervously, Many had asked if he could
speak to her about an important matter, then knelt by the table where she
was sitting and spoke to her in a quiet voice.

'Do you know how I gave evidence against Tom Domican?' said Many.

'Not really, but sort of,' Johnson had replied.

'Well, the evidence that I gave wasn't true and I want to tell the truth; I
really want to set the record straight but I'm afraid if I do so Ron Woodham
would have me killed,' said Many, according to the evidence Ms Johnson
gave to the court. Woodham was the head of the prison's Internal
Investigations Unit at the time, dealing with tough and duplicitous
prisoners, and has since been promoted with no stain on his professional
record.

Many told Johnson he wanted to make a statement about it but he
wanted her first to guarantee his safety. She told him she would see what she
could do. However when she next visited the gaol, he had been moved to
another protection area. It was next to the prison hospital and inmates were
identified only by number. She decided against asking to see him for his own
safety.

In an equally unusual move, the three judges on the Court of Criminal
Appeal called Many before them to be questioned about Johnson's
allegations. Put on the spot by the state's highest court, Many had to deal
with five different stories.

In story number one, he told the court it was Johnson who had
approached him and not the other way around. He said she asked him to
retract the evidence he had given against Domican in the Vandenburg trial,
which he said he had refused to agree to. He claimed Johnson gave him an
ounce of heroin as a 'token' of Domican's goodwill—this was a lie. He
hadn't used the heroin and said he had flushed it right down the toilet
although he acknowledged that within the prison system, heroin was a
valuable, tradeable commodity. This was Many, the upstanding citizen,
trying to impress their Honours on the bench.

In story number two, it emerged that immediately after the meeting with Johnson in April 1989, Many had written a statement along the lines of the conversation she said he had with her, saying he was afraid of Woodham.

Story number three involved an interview within the special protection prison in December 1989 with prosecutors who had confronted Many with the claims made by Johnson. In that interview, Many at first denied he even knew her, then said he could not recall meeting her, then denied that, in any conversation they might have had, Domican's name was ever mentioned.

In story four, Many swore an affidavit in January 1990 in which he said he had spoken to Johnson about legal books and it was she who asked him to retract the evidence he had given against Domican. There was no mention of heroin, nor was there any mention of the money which emerged in fairytale number five.

In his fifth story, in February 1990, he had sworn yet another affidavit in which he claimed Johnson had offered him money to change his story and had also offered to get him Domican's solicitor to conduct his appeal.

The judges didn't believe him. Justice Michael Kirby, who was at the time acting chief justice of New South Wales and has since moved to the High Court, said Johnson had no ostensible reason for lying about her conversation with Many. He said Many's conflicting versions of the events went to the very heart of the truth of what he had said at the trial. He said there was a sufficiently real possibility that a jury would acquit Domican and Drummond hearing this fresh evidence. The court also noted that during cross-examination during the Vandenburg trial, Many had admitted he had committed perjury in another trial, the trial of Kevin Gallagher for the murder of a fellow prisoner in the early 1980s. The murder at Parramatta Gaol in the early 1980s about which Many had given key evidence had finally came back to haunt him. The NSW Court of Criminal Appeal quashed the convictions of Domican and Drummond for the Vandenburg conspiracy and ordered retrials.

Strike two.

Then something happened that was truly amazing. Mum and I had moved to a beautiful terraced house in a quiet tree lined street in an inner city suburb of Sydney. Many was never far from our minds but we knew he was locked away and unable to hurt anyone else. In December 1990, as we were looking forward to spending Christmas with family and friends, the court that recognised Many's unreliable evidence, the NSW Court of Criminal Appeal, although constituted by three different judges, made a decision that threw our lives into turmoil once again. The court slashed Many's sentence for the rape and attack on me—as his reward for being a prison informer. This was the same man the court had just a few months earlier branded a liar in the Vandenburg matter. It seems that apart from Many himself, there was no-one in the system who knew what the other hand was doing. I would have thought that at least someone in the Office of the New South Wales Director of Public Prosecutions, who had lawyers appearing in each of these appeals, should have had an overview of what was going on. They didn't.

Many had initially lodged an appeal against his seven convictions but dropped that on the day he got to the Appeal Court. He continued only with his appeal against the sentence. His lawyer, paid for by Legal Aid, had argued that had Justice Carruthers been told, at the time he sentenced Many, how much help Many had been to the various authorities, he would have imposed a lesser sentence. At the time, there were well-established legal precedents that said informers should be rewarded with lesser sentences. On top of that, speaking up for him in the Court of Criminal Appeal in favour of a sentence reduction were officers from no less than the National Crime Authority, the New South Wales Police and the New South Wales Department of Corrective Services' Internal Investigations Unit at Long Bay Gaol. Not only that, the Crown, represented by a prosecutor from the Director of Public Prosecution's office, did not oppose Many's appeal. The Department of Corrective Services told the court what a tough time Many was having in the special protection section of the gaol. They said the restrictions of being in protection could have an 'adverse effect on his family and friends so far as restrictions concerning gaol visits and their personal safety'. No mention of the extra phone calls and the conjugal visits that other prisoners in the mainstream did not enjoy, nor of that electronic keyboard.

Incredibly, the Appeal Court, constituted by Justice Mervyn Finlay, Justice Colin Allen and Justice Jeremy Badgery-Parker, said:

'It appears from the material now before the court that (Many) at no stage sought to use his willingness to inform and give evidence at great risk to himself and to his family to bargain in any way for benefits.

'He did not act out of self-interest. What has been his motivation? Certainly what he did was not a manifestation of contrition in respect of the crimes for which he came to be sentenced in March 1988. There is no evidence that he ever expressed contrition for those appalling crimes.

'Whatever his motivations, the fact of his significant and substantial assistance in respect of serious crime is to be given just as much credit by way of discount whether such crime is within the prison system or in the community generally.'

But the line that really hurts from the judgment is: 'The overriding duty of this court is to avoid a miscarriage of justice.'

What! The court, by cutting his sentence, achieved completely the opposite. The court was told that Many had refused to give evidence in the committal proceedings involving the Flannery murder but as his action was attributed to the refusal of the court to suppress his identity, it was excused. No-one told the court, and amazingly the court apparently did not know because the judges certainly did not mention it, that just nine months earlier their brother judges sitting in those very same seats had quashed the convictions of two people because they ruled Many had been an unreliable witness, a liar. The three judges in their joint judgment quoted a High Court decision which set a precedent for rewarding prison informers with reduced sentences. In the decision, the High Court had said: 'What is to be encouraged is full and frank co-operation on the part of the offender whatever be his motive … The information must, of course, be true: a false disclosure attracts no discount at all.'

Many's information turned out to be all lies—not 'full and frank' at all.

The court was also under the misapprehension that Many had been a help to society by saving the life of the prison governor, Peter Bruce, in 1986—the truth of what had really happened was still a secret known only to Many and Raymond Hornby.

As it turned out, contrary to what Many's lawyer had said to the Appeal Court, before sentencing Many, Justice Carruthers had been told he was an informer and was due to give evidence in several matters, however he had not mentioned that in his sentencing remarks. The Court of Criminal Appeal said that on the face of it, it appeared the judge had not taken it into account when sentencing Many to twenty years in gaol. Yet the Appeal Court said in the same breath that Justice Carruthers 'may' have felt he need not have given Many any benefit for that because he had already received a benefit in getting out of gaol early from his previous sentence. He had also had more than seven years' parole revoked on his previous sentence, which would seem to be not an insubstantial benefit.

The Appeal Court did its sums and found that with what was then an automatic one-third discount off the sentences of all prisoners for good behaviour (a discount we did not know about and which no longer happens under truth in sentencing legislation in New South Wales) Many would be spending just under thirteen years in gaol. As a reward for informing, they took off some more. Many's twenty-year sentence had been slashed to just eight and a half years.

He had played the system and won.

Thankfully, the media jumped on the injustice. On Wednesday, 12 December, Mum and I were rushing through breakfast in our usual morning routine as we got ready for work when we received a telephone call from a radio journalist that Mum had worked with. He told us that in a newspaper that morning was the story about what the Court of Criminal Appeal had done. It meant Many would be back on the streets in five years' time. When we hung up the phone, Mum and I sank down into chairs, trying to understand what we had just been told. To say we were devastated does not describe how we felt. We felt total disbelief and then anger. No sooner had we started to take in the news than the phone began ringing with people who worked in the media and who knew Mum and me personally. The reporters wanted me to talk about it in the newspapers and on TV and radio. Mum answered all the calls and asked me how I felt about speaking out. It was not something I had ever thought about but I felt the system had turned its back on Mum and me. Mum's feeling was that we were honest people and we could not let this kind of injustice happen. She said we had the choice of just letting it go and keeping quiet and getting on with our lives—or fighting it. I was not feeling confident about giving interviews but we decided to go ahead and fight it. It was from this moment on that I would become identified in the media as 'Fred Many's victim'.

Mum and I were in a tailspin but once again, we tried to do the right thing by everyone, including the media. We gave as many interviews as we possibly could in the hope we could persuade the court to change its mind. I felt the judges had made a mockery of everything Mum and I had been through and achieved.

In the newspapers, the case was given front page treatment and it made headline news on television. The media respected the security which still surrounded Mum and me and my identity was disguised. I had to appear either in shadow or was filmed from behind. The case also filled talkback radio. Kathryn Greiner took it up on the programme she then had on the radio station 2UE. I gave her an interview on radio and she was very kind and gentle towards me. Her involvement was significant because of who she was married to—Nick Greiner, the then New South Wales Premier. She went on to interview her husband's Attorney-General, John Dowd.

In what was a heated interview, Kathryn Greiner asked Mr Dowd to justify the reasons for the court's decision. Mr Dowd said he did not need to justify it because it was not a decision of the government. He dismissed suggestions the government should be more selective about which prisoners were used as informers, saying the Crown 'can't be fussy about who their witnesses are'. The judges, he said, had done the right thing by applying the law.

Kathryn Greiner asked him why prisoners should be treated differently to other citizens who were required to give information without expecting any reward for it. He replied that a prisoner who turned informer was subject to harsher conditions for his own protection and therefore needed a reward as a carrot to come forward. Kathryn Greiner had the final say: 'I'm sorry, Mr Dowd, I'm not interested. If he has to be hung up by his toenails for three months it wouldn't be enough. Why don't you think about it for a moment from the young girl's point of view please? He has ruined her life and she requires psychiatric help. Now, that whole process will stay with her for the rest of her life.'

I was feeling very much like a fish out of water during this time. I still could not understand how it had happened and was trying to keep myself together enough to fight it and not fall apart. I had been left feeling completely beaten; beaten by Many, beaten by the courts, beaten by the whole justice system. It was the justice system that had allowed Many out of gaol in the first place in 1986 even though he had not gone anywhere close to serving his initial sentence. They released him early from gaol and less than seven weeks later he had attacked me. Yet again, here was the system preparing to release him back into society early before he had served the sentence he had been given. He had been responsible for twice trying to kill me on the night of 2 September, had placed a contract on my life and Mum's life which carried enough of a threat to warrant police protection yet now he was being given another chance. Just as Mum and I were managing to pick up the pieces of our lives, Fred Many had managed to rip our security away again.

We had our solicitor get in contact with the Office of the New South Wales Director of Public Prosecutions and write to the Attorney-General, Mr Dowd, urging them to appeal against the decision to the High Court. Appeals to the High Court are not automatic and first the court has to agree to hear the appeal. With the weight of public opinion in our favour, the Crown did seek special leave to appeal to the High Court against Many's sentence reduction. However the court sent them packing, saying that because they had not opposed the reduction in the first place in the Court of Criminal Appeal, then they couldn't turn around and do it later. Fred Many would be released from gaol on 4 March 1995 and there was nothing more we could do about it.

The news that Many's sentence reduction was going to stand nearly broke Mum and me. Everything I had gone through seemed to have been for nothing and I found myself wishing for the first time that I had never gone to the police and that I had just tried to continue with my life. At least then none of this would have happened and I wouldn't have put Mum through the hell we had experienced. However I knew that if I hadn't reported the attack, I wouldn't have been Many's last victim. He could have gone on to attack other little girls.

Mum and I were back in touch with the witness protection group who told us that security surrounding us would be stepped up when Many was released. They also brought up the prospect of changing our identities so Many would never be able to track us down but Mum and I were determined not to allow the police to do that. Many had taken away so much, we refused to let him take away our identities as well.

We still knew very little about what Many had been doing behind the scenes to pull off his coup but it later became clear that his career as a prison informer in the witness boxes of the state's courts was by then all over. The public disgust as well as the subsequent inquiry conducted by the New South Wales Independent Commission Against Corruption in 1992 into the use of informers saw to that. Despite all the 'help' he was supposed to have been to society, Many was considered so unreliable that he was never to give evidence in a courtroom again.

In April 1992, the NSW Director of Public Prosecutions dropped the charges against Tom Domican and Peter Drummond relating to the Vandenburg conspiracy. There was to be no retrial.

Strike three.

In May 1992, the High Court quashed Tom Domican's September 1988 conviction for the attempted murders of the Flannery family and ordered a new trial.

Strike Four.

A few days later, Domican was granted bail and after five-and-a-half years spent in maximum security prisons around the state, he had his first taste of freedom. Holding the hand of his wife, Ellen, who had stood by him throughout, he went off to see his daughters who were aged only one and two when he had been gaoled in 1986.

Soon after, the Director of Public Prosecutions dropped the charges of attempting to murder Flannery and his family and, not long after, dropped the final charge against Domican of conspiring to murder the former police officer, Max Gudgeon.

Strikes five and six.

The outcome was that Many's evidence had led to not one safe conviction in any court. He had managed to make his life in gaol as comfortable as he could and had received the ultimate reward of getting out of gaol early for no actual benefit to the justice system at all. And his dream run was still not over. During the ICAC inquiry, there was yet more evidence that he had lied. A Community Corrections Officer told ICAC that back in April 1989, Many had complained to her that the police had not helped him as they had promised. He had turned on his minders, telling her that the evidence he had given in the courts had been a 'script', written for him by the police. The timing of this was significant because it was about the same time that Leigh Johnson said he had told her much the same story.

ICAC commissioner, Ian Temby, said in his report: 'Before me, Many denied having said that, but could offer no reason why [the Community Corrections Officer] would lie about it. It is also noted that [the officer's] evidence is consistent with that given to the Court of Criminal Appeal by the solicitor, Johnson, to the effect that Many had told her his evidence at the trial was false.'

However no charges were recommended against Many for his perjury. It also angered me that those people who lied for him at his trial, saying they were with him on the day he attacked me or claimed I was Many's girlfriend, were never to face perjury charges either.

Meanwhile there had been developments in Many's personal life. He had fallen out with Robyn, who had decided she wanted nothing more to do with him, and there was a new woman in his life, Barbara, a divorcee with two young children—both girls, aged six and eight. The girls were not much younger than the two girls Many had tried to abduct before he kidnapped me. Barbara was one of those people who believe they can do good by visiting prisoners which was how she had met the new love of her life. In 1994, she became the next Mrs Fred Many in yet another gaol wedding.

So all that hard work Many had put in—from telling Lyndie Cashman to search the files at Gosford Library to writing those long letters to police officers and those hours he spent going over his evidence in prison so he could then sit in witness boxes for days on end—had been worth it from his point of view.

He might have become public enemy number one along the way but no matter how long and hard people shouted from now on, he knew there was nothing they could do to stand in his way. He was home and dry and he had not only stayed within the law, he had done it all with the help of the legal system. He knew that on 4 March 1995 he would walk out of gaol, with his latest wife waiting for him and not even the threat of parole hanging over his head.

His gamble had paid off.

CHAPTER 13

THE EXILE

I had to leave the country. The thought of Fred Many being back on the streets so soon was almost too much to bear. Not a day went by that Mum and I were not worrying about what would happen when he was released. We felt we were not living our lives: we were just waiting.

My girlfriend, Alison, was planning a trip to Europe and Mum and I felt it would be better if I went with her to distance myself from further danger. I could not get much further away than the other side of the world. Leaving Australia had never been an option before as it meant I would be leaving behind Mum and the close and special relationship we had come to share. I started to entertain the idea as a way of keeping not just myself out of danger, but of lessening the risk to Mum. It was me who Many really wanted and with me out of the country, it would be harder for him to find Mum.

I discussed the plan with John and Grahame and they were in favour. However they wanted me to take an even more drastic step. The two of them and their bosses in the witness protection programme insisted I change my name so Many would not be able to come after me overseas. It made me feel vulnerable and scared all over again. It reinforced the threat from Many was real and unnerving if they thought he had the kind of contacts that could track me down through my passport. While just a few months earlier I had put my foot down and refused to change my identity, I now felt beaten. I felt I had little choice but to agree. I don't know about the intricacies of how they went about getting all the official paperwork needed for my new identity but the process began when Grahame gave me a normal passport application and asked me to fill it in. I had to put down a different name and we sat down together and thought up a new name for me, a bizarre task—I could have called myself anything I wanted, however I wasn't really in the mood to make silly suggestions. A few days later, Grahame presented me with an Australian passport in my new name together with a birth certificate and a new Medicare card. The process had been so thorough that even the names of my parents had been changed on my new birth certificate. I had ceased to be Kirstyn Austin.

As we planned the trip, Mum, my gran and my aunts and uncles pretended it was a holiday for me. No-one wanted to discuss the fact that it was because of Many that I was going. But we all knew that I was not coming back. I knew I would be leaving Mum to cope with Many's release alone but she convinced me she would be OK and Grahame assured me that if anything happened, he would look after her for me. Meanwhile, Mum and I spent as much time together as we could, as if we could build up a store of love and hugs to draw on when we were apart.

I was awake as dawn broke on the day I was to leave for London in early 1991. It had been almost five years since the attack and how my life had changed. While I could have expected to have completed school, perhaps gone to university or started to build a career, like most other twenty-year-olds, here I was living a life on the run.

I had to be at the airport by 12.30 p.m. to check in for my flight. Mum had gone to work that morning but had arranged to meet me at the airport. My cousin, Grayson, had been visiting us and was trying his best to keep my spirits up that morning but I was feeling acutely aware of the consequences of leaving and, even worse, the possibility of never coming back. I was dressed and ready quite early but ended up repacking everything, double-checking I had forgotten nothing. I stopped and cried many times as I looked around the comfortable little home Mum and I had created together.

The sense of security our home gave me was slowly but surely ebbing away and already I was feeling very alone.

Another friend, Sonya, was coming to the airport with me. The cab arrived, I was ready to go and my bags were placed in the boot. But before I could leave, I had to turn for one last look at the house. I took a photograph to remind me of the times I had shared there with Mum. There were good-byes to say on the way to the airport as I called into the place where I had worked because I wanted to say a final farewell to everyone. Again, I was in tears. These people had been so wonderful to me since we had heard about Many's early release and had given me all the time I needed off work to speak to the police, our solicitor and to organise this trip. I would not have been able to get through everything without their support and I thanked them for that.

When we got to the airport, there was Mum waiting for us at the taxi stand. We held each other tightly, both crying already although I had a couple of hours to go before the plane left. I looked around at my other friends who were there and felt lucky to know such people. One face I couldn't see was Dad's. I had given him the details of the flight and told him what time we would be at the airport but I hadn't heard back from him and didn't know whether he would be coming to say goodbye. Since he and Mum had divorced, I hadn't seen as much of him as I had wanted.

Alison, her mum Rosemary and some other friends and family were waiting in the bar in the international terminal. It turned out that there was quite a large gathering. I tried to stretch out the time as much as possible but it couldn't go on forever. Finally came the time to go through into the passenger-only waiting area. It was time to say goodbye. At that final doorway leading to immigration and customs, Alison and I stood together surrounded by our families and friends. It was as if we were the only people in the airport, we were so focused on saying farewell. This was where the tears really flowed. Mum and I held on to each other as long as we could. She was the last person I said goodbye to and the one I came back for. Alison had waved goodbye and walked through the doorway and behind the screens. I took a few steps to follow her towards the man waiting to take my hand luggage and put it through the scanner but I couldn't do it. I grabbed my hand luggage back, turned and bolted back through the door and out to Mum. I really felt as though something was being ripped from me physically. Mum and I had been through so much together that the thought of not having her around sent chills down my spine. I knew this was the last time I was to see her for many, many years. We gripped each other so tightly that not even a cyclone could have parted us—but Fred Many was doing just that. I can still remember crying into Mum's shoulder and smelling her hair. It was the same comforting smell I remembered as a child and would wake from a bad dream to smell as she hugged me and soothed me back to sleep.

After all I had been through, that day was the worst of my life. I was leaving home secretly like a criminal with my world in a suitcase while Many basked in the extra privileges he had received by becoming a prison informer. Where was the justice in that? I gathered myself together, said a final farewell and headed back to join Alison and into a new life where I didn't know what I was going to do or what I could expect.

I didn't expect it to be as bad as it was. My time in London was bleak to say the least. Alison and I started off in a dingy hotel, then moved to the YWCA. She soon left to travel through Europe and I found myself living under an unfamiliar name in a foreign country, away from my family and knowing not a soul. I had very little money and the little I had managed to save soon ran out. I tried obtaining temp work while living in an outer suburb of London but the work was too irregular and I could not make enough to live off. I got a job as a barmaid in a nightclub and rented a cheap one-bedroom flat which was not only tiny but also cold and damp. The money I was able to earn at the club was cut by half because after each night at work, I had to take a cab home. I refused to take the trains during the deserted early hours of the morning.

As one of the cab company's most regular customers, I got to know the lady who answered the company's phones quite well and she would try to send me the same driver each night to pick me up. It was a huge relief when I was able to recognise the driver as it gave me a sense of security. I started to get to know the driver, whose name was Shawn, and after a few months he asked me out for dinner. I didn't give him an answer straight away because I was still feeling extremely vulnerable and wasn't sure about the idea of going out on a date with anyone at that stage. Shawn saw me to my front door that night and accepted the fact that I needed time to think. I went inside that dismal flat and thought about the idea of going out to dinner with a man I barely knew. The alarm bells were going off in my head and all kinds of worst-case scenarios were going through my mind. However I gave it a lot of thought that night. I decided that I had to start moving on and start living the life of a normal twenty-year-old. The following night when Shawn picked me up from work, I took a deep breath and told him I would accept his offer of dinner.

That decision turned out to be yet another mistake I would make.

Initially the relationship between Shawn and me flourished and we were soon seeing each other on a regular basis. I saw him as a kind, gentle man who would look after me which was what I thought I needed. He tried his best to show me around, help me to get to know the area and to feel more at ease. When we reached a stage in our relationship where I felt I had to tell him about my past, I found it very difficult for me but it would not be until much later that I would learn how much more difficult it was for Shawn. I had been desperately lonely in London and terribly afraid and so I fell in love with Shawn for all the wrong reasons. Here for me was someone who I thought would care for me and give me the same feeling of safety I had from John and Grahame in witness protection. It was not to be.

Then I accidentally fell pregnant. Shawn really wanted to have the baby and went so far as to ask me to marry him. In my need for security, I accepted and we were married in June the following year. My beautiful little boy Ben was born and gave me such a sense of achievement. I felt that now I was not just 'Many's victim' as portrayed in the media but a wife and a mother and I gripped my new role with both hands.

The other side of all that was that Mum could not share it with me. Getting married and giving birth to Ben away from Mum and my family was the loneliest experience. I really needed Mum during the first two years of Ben's life. I needed her to reassure me that I was doing the right thing by way of caring for him, to be a friend and to do all the 'mum' things, but we could not afford me going home to Australia or for Mum to visit us in London. Even the cost of calling Australia was so high that we had to make do with five-minute telephone conversations at Christmas and birthdays, conversations that were at the same time difficult, cheerful and heart-breaking. Around the time Mum knew Ben was due to be born, she had sat by the phone for days waiting to hear word and when I called to tell her the good news, we spoke and cried for about an hour. That was a rare exception. I know Mum felt as robbed as I did that she was not with me during that time.

Shawn had turned into a different person after we got married and we had lots of rows. That is not to say there were not still some good times. But finally things came to a stage where I felt I couldn't continue to live the life I had stumbled into and made the decision to leave. Three times Shawn and I split up and each time he persuaded me things would be different. We would get back together but we would soon end up having arguments over the same old things. My true joy at that time was my son. He kept me going.

In March 1995, Shawn and I were back together for the third time. Ben had turned two in October 1994. That winter in London was dreadfully cold with the winds blowing across from Russia. We woke every morning to ice on the windows inside, as well as ice on the ground outside. It was bitterly cold and so very bleak. My thoughts were turning to Australia constantly and not because of the sunshine I had left behind. It was because of Many and his impending release. I knew he was due to walk out of gaol sometime that month but was not sure of the exact date. I tried not to dwell on the knowledge he would soon be free but it was during one of those freezing cold nights that the call came.

When a phone rings in the middle of the night, it really is no wonder why we automatically think it is bad news—it usually is. When the phone woke me up, I raced from the bedroom into the lounge room to pick it up before it woke Ben, who had been suffering from a cold. It was Mum and her voice was shaking on the other end of the line. I knew something was wrong. In my rush to get to the phone, I hadn't stopped to put on anything warmer than the shirt and socks I had been wearing in bed but the news Mum had for me would send a chill through me that even the thickest dressing gown and warmest slippers could not have stopped.

She started by having a general conversation along the lines of how we both were, that sort of thing—but at two-thirty in the morning, I knew that was not the real reason for her call. I finally asked what was wrong. It was Fred Many, she said. He was to be released at the end of the week, on Saturday, 4 March. I couldn't believe it had come around so soon. I had somehow hoped that he would have to serve more time in prison. It was not to be the case. Mum went on to say that the media at home had once again picked up on the case and because Many's impending release had coincided with the New South Wales election, which was also being held that Saturday, the politicians had been drawn into the controversy Many's release was generating and were all trying to score points against each other in the pre-election campaign.

The controversy had indeed taken off and was gathering weight like a snowball speeding down a mountainside. I couldn't believe what I was hearing. One of the most disturbing reports had been in the *Australian* that Wednesday. It revealed how the police had reopened their investigation into the disappearance nine years earlier of the Sydney schoolgirl Samantha Knight, aged nine. I had remembered reading about her at the time, just before I was attacked. Over the years, her disappearance had generated more publicity than any other missing person in Australian history. She had last been seen near her home in Bondi on 19 August 1986, during the short few weeks Many had last been out of gaol and two weeks before he attacked me. Many's ex-wife, Lyndie Cashman—who was to emerge a hero for what she did—told the newspaper that she had been interviewed by police some years earlier about Many's whereabouts on the day Samantha Knight went missing. She knew that he had the use of her car that day and had said he was going to Sydney. The police were quoted as saying they believed Samantha bore a striking resemblance to myself—we were both young, slightly built and blonde. 'They could have been sisters,' said one of the officers. When she had been spoken to by police, Lyndie had told them that while Many had been back in gaol in 1986, he had asked her to go to a site east of Katoomba in the Blue Mountains which was distinguishable by certain landmarks. He had told her he had some money buried there but when she went there, she found it to be dense bushland and was scared so she never dug for anything. She said that she did not know what else he might have had buried there.

Mum said that over the next few days, all hell had broken loose. The statement Raymond Hornby had written in gaol years earlier revealing Many's 'rescue' of the prison superintendent Peter Bruce as a sham had been handed to journalist Janet Fife-Yeomans by the prisoner whom Hornby had entrusted it to. She gave it prominent publicity and the statement was passed on to police. They began investigating a charge of perverting the course of justice against Many. It was significant that although Hornby had told police about the sham rescue back in 1991, no action had been taken against Many at that time. Once again, it took the media to pull together what the law enforcement authorities should have been investigating.

Then Lyndie Cashman told police a secret she had kept for eight and a half years. During that short burst of freedom in 1986, Many had robbed a liquor store and a corner store in the Sydney suburbs of Neutral Bay and Croydon. Many had asked Lyndie to get rid of the weapons he had used. She had been afraid to come forward before for fear of being charged with being an accessory to the robberies. She had not given him up to police at the time, now, promised immunity from prosecution, Lyndie told police all she knew. She even offered to undergo hypnosis if it would help her to remember more details.

By the Thursday morning, the then New South Wales Premier John

Fahey had cancelled all public engagements at what was the most crucial part of his re-election campaign as he held crisis talks with the police and his Attorney-General's Department. A team of nine detectives from the special crime unit of the major crime squad had been set up to investigate the flood of fresh evidence against Many. There were the two armed robberies, the Bruce matter and, after Tom Domican became involved, there were the charges of falsely accusing somebody of a crime. After waiting a long time for his revenge, Domican spent two hours with detectives detailing why Many should face criminal charges for the lies he had told in the witness box.

With two days to go until Many's release, the police were, literally, working around the clock. They drove to Goulburn Gaol to interview Many but he refused to answer questions. They interviewed Hornby. They took Lyndie Cashman from the Central Coast to Sydney to see if she could identify the places Many had said he had robbed. She could—and there had indeed been robberies reported at those two premises at the time. The police spoke to the victims of the robberies and they corroborated Lyndie's claims. Their descriptions of the robber matched Many.

John Davidson, who had by then retired from the New South Wales Police Service, also became involved. He publicly warned that Many was 'an animal, a maniac ... wild, violent and unpredictable'. As blunt as ever, he dismissed as 'crap' suggestions the police had protected Many but revealed that when, based on Many's word, the NCA had charged Tom Domican with murdering Christopher Flannery, the NCA knew he hadn't done it. Detective Davidson had not been involved in charging Domican with that matter. As a sign of how times had changed, the former police officer also said the only thing he had regretted in twenty-five years in the police force was being party to Many's application to the New South Wales Court of Criminal Appeal which led to his sentence being reduced. He said it was the most distasteful matter he had been involved with during his police career.

The legal experts were asked how Many could be kept in gaol in lieu of fresh charges. While the legal academics said it would raise serious moral issues and differed on whether it would be right or wrong, they seemed to agree that it would be both possible and constitutional for the government to pass special legislation designed specifically to keep Many in gaol. One suggested a more civil libertarian approach would be for a judge to review Many's sentence and reconsider any remissions he had received if they had been received under false pretences.

But time was running out. So strong was the public reaction that the New South Wales Liberal Government spent almost $50,000 on a newspaper advertising campaign explaining why it had no alternative but to allow Many to walk free. As politicians do, they blamed other politicians. They said it was the fault of the previous Labor Government for making the laws under which Many's sentence had been cut.

Then Many, who had been reading, listening and watching all this in his prison cell, released a statement through a Legal Aid lawyer. He denied any involvement with Samantha Knight, questioned the motives of Lyndie Cashman in helping police, said his sentence was lawful and could not be attacked now. He said if there was to be any investigation into anything involving him, it should be done by 'proper police procedure' and not conducted publicly through the media.

In the midst of this whirlwind was Mum. Because I was out of the country and my whereabouts were known only to Mum, she had been doing the interviews on my behalf. Once again she had been appearing only in shadow because it was by then even more essential her identity and the city she lived in be protected with Many getting out of gaol in a matter of days. She had tried to explain to people the double dealing that had gone on and she had been fighting on her own to try to stop Many's release. It tore my heart out to know Mum was all alone in Australia. I was also upset because all the details of the case would be written about again, that people would be reminded about the things Many did to me and that all I would be, once again, was 'Many's victim'. I didn't have a name, I was not a real person, I was this man's 'victim'.

Mum asked if I wanted to do anything or if there was anything in particular that I thought should be done. We spoke about how totally and absolutely disgusted I was with the outcome of all the hard work we had put in only to see Many walk free after eight-and-a-half years.

Mum asked me how I would feel about giving an interview to the television programme, *60 Minutes*. She said they had been speaking to her and were really interested in the case. They already had a reporter and a producer on an international flight to London in the hope I would give them an interview, although she had not given them my address or told them my new identity. I was completely taken aback and naturally I was extremely hesitant. It wasn't that I didn't want my views to be known but *60 Minutes* wanted me to appear on camera with no shadows, no digital cover over my face—they wanted me to appear as who I was. I desperately needed to think about it but I had so little time if I was to make a difference. Not only was the crew on the way but more importantly, Many was getting out a minute after midnight, the early hours of Saturday, 4 March, just as he had been promised by the law courts and the judges. There was a not lot of time left.

We talked it over and Mum was understandably very concerned about me appearing on camera. However I was so very angry that Fred Many could do the things he did and get away with them. I was fed up with only being known as the 'victim' and as the shadowy figure in newspapers or on the television news. I felt very strongly that I wanted people to see me as a real person, as the young girl I was, and to be able to identify with what happened to me. After all this time and no matter what distance I put between him and myself, Many still had the ability to manipulate my life. I was also acutely conscious that watching the interview would be Many himself. I decided to do it. The time for the interview was set for Friday and it was not until during the interview that I realised that with the time difference, I would be speaking to the interviewer, Richard Carleton, at the same time as Many walked out of Long Bay Gaol. The interview was set to take place at a hotel off Sloane Square used by the *60 Minutes* crew when in London. I was still cautious about them knowing exactly where I lived—or my real name. We chose the pseudonym of Susan for the interview.

It was a big moment for me and I wanted to look my best so that morning I went to the hairdressers to try to have something done with what was then a mess of permed hair. The hairdresser failed and I walked out of there looking like a French poodle was sitting on my head. I had to laugh. There I was about to show myself to friends and family who had not seen me for years as well as people who did not even know me and had never seen me before and I looked like I had put my finger in an electric socket.

I wanted to make a good impression and had a suit which I saved for special occasions so I wore it for the interview. It was certainly a special occasion. Despite my preparations, when I got there I was a bundle of nerves. My hands had taken on a life of their own, they were shaking in my lap, in fact every limb of my body was shaking. I had heard of Richard Carleton's reputation for being very critical and quite ruthless and I had no idea whether he would see the whole case in the same light as I did. As it turned out, I had nothing to worry about. He was very kind and his questions were gentle and respectful, something I thanked him for. On ending the interview, Richard asked me a question which summed up the whole situation. He asked: 'Who got the life sentence?'

I answered: 'You're looking at her.'

When the time came to say goodbye to Richard Carleton and the *60 Minutes* crew, it was strange but it was quite an emotional leave-taking for me. Although I had only known them for a few hours, they were a link to home. I felt I was again leaving Australia behind. They were fortunate enough to be returning to Australia whereas I had only a small flat in Surrey to return to. I felt as if once again any connection with my real home was being severed. It was hard to walk away and not beg them to take me with them.

Shawn had accompanied me to the interview and on our way back to Surrey, I kept asking him what he thought about the interview. Did I sound OK? Did I sound foolish? Did I say anything stupid? Did I make sense? It was important to me that I had not come across as sounding like a fool and that I had made the points I needed to make and had made them clearly.

Shawn said I had done just fine. While steering the car with one hand, he patted me on the knee with the other and said it was now all over and we should get back to normal. His comment threw me into a spin. I couldn't understand how I could possibly continue to act as if nothing had happened. As of that moment, Many was free from gaol. For all we knew, he still wanted me dead and Shawn wanted to get back to 'normal'. Our relationship diminished irreparably from that point on.

The *60 Minutes* interview aired on the Sunday night, too late to do anything to stop Many getting out. He had walked free to an extraordinary media coverage. The television and radio stations carried live crosses as he left Long Bay Gaol just after midnight on the Friday night. He sped off in a white car to live with his new wife, Barbara, and her two little girls in a flat in the Sydney suburb of Paddington. They soon moved to a house in Bathurst, near Many's family.

It was some months before I was to see the TV footage of that night and when I did, I saw that Many looked much older than when he attacked me but he still had the ability to fill me with fear and loathing. The *60 Minutes* people told me that the interview had been the highest-rating episode of the programme for the whole year.

Another person who was interviewed by *60 Minutes* was Detective Davidson. He also did an interview with another TV current affairs pro-gramme, both, he said, on the condition that the fees he negotiated be sent direct to the rape crisis centre at Royal Prince Alfred Hospital in Sydney. He wanted the money to be used to buy clothes for the rape victims because their clothes are often taken away by police to be examined and are kept to be used as exhibits.

While the police investigation into the armed robbery charges continued, the New South Wales Director of Public Prosecutions (DPP), Nicholas Cowdery QC, had decided not to prosecute Many for the conspiracy to pervert the course of justice over the 'rescue' of Peter Bruce and the perjury involving Tom Domican. The reason, he said, was because of the unreliable nature of evidence of the people who had made statements against him.

Raymond Hornby, he said, had a lengthy criminal history including murder. He said he was concerned about the authenticity of the contents of that statement he had made in gaol over the 'rescue', although he went on to say that it had not been the first time Hornby had spoken of the 'rescue' as a hoax. He had done so to the NSW Supreme Court around the time of making the statement in 1991 when he had applied for a redetermination of his life sentence. The DPP said that Hornby's statement, if authentic, added little. When I read that later, it seemed to me very wrong that just because action was not taken earlier, it could not be taken then. In the words of the old cliché, two wrongs do not make a right. The evidence of another prisoner against Many was also dismissed because of the prisoner's criminal history and because he had refused to give evidence on the subject before.

As for Lyndie Cashman, her evidence was dismissed by the DPP because she had not, at that time, signed a statement; because she was his former wife and because she was 'an associate of known criminals'. The 'known criminals' were solely her sister, Julie—hardly the fault of Lyndie. It was significant that she not only went on to make a statement but was ready to give evidence against Many at his trial.

The view taken by the DPP in 1995 was a completely different view to that taken by his predecessor, the former DPP, in all the trials in which Many had been used as a witness. He had a lengthy criminal history, he was an associate of known criminals and the authenticity of his evidence was questionable—yet he had been put up as a witness of truth time and time again. The changes that had come about in the justice system, predominantly because of the publicity surrounding Many, had turned into a double-edged sword. Because of the Many factor, the DPP would no longer rely on the testimony of prison informers—and it was ironic that such a change was to benefit one of Australia's most prolific and notorious prison informers, Fred Many. It struck me all over again how unfair the justice system could be.

Shawn could never understand how all this had affected me, or the fear I felt with Many being out of gaol. Even though I was at the other side of the world with a new identity, he still scared me. For the next few days after he was released, I did my best to do what Shawn suggested and tried to behave as if nothing had happened but it was impossible. Every time I went out, I looked over my shoulder again. I walked around with my head down in case I caught someone's eye and somehow they recognised me. Every time the phone rang, I thought it would be bad news from Australia—that Many had found Mum. She had called me after seeing the *60 Minutes* programme and told me how proud she was of me and how well she thought the interview had gone. It was also the first time she had 'seen' me other than in photographs since I left home so it was especially meaningful to both of us. I was missing her all over again.

However money was still tight for both Mum and me so the telephone calls had to stop once again. It was back to waiting for Christmas and birthdays. We were left at opposite ends of the world to ponder alone on what had happened. It was a very difficult time for me. Shawn and I separated for the final time. Months passed and I felt more and more homesick with every day. I could not stop thinking that Many was out there walking the streets openly and freely where he chose and was living with his family back in Australia while I was living in London completely isolated from everyone I loved and cared for. I felt myself going downhill quickly.

CHAPTER 14

THE HOMECOMING

It was on one of those dismal days that the telephone rang once again in the early hours of the morning. I knew it was Mum and expected the worst as I picked up the handset. This time, she was bubbling with excitement. The news was good, very good. She had managed to save up enough money to pay for a ticket to get me home. I couldn't believe what she was telling me and was so overwhelmed that for a moment I could not speak. Mum said she hadn't been able to stand the fact that I was so alone and that we couldn't see each other. Suddenly the world looked like a better, brighter place. The happiness I felt was indescribable. I felt I was now going to be released from my own prison cell.

We wasted no time. Within a week Ben and I were on a plane heading for Brisbane. Mum had moved there into a small flat since I had left for England. She hadn't been able to tell me straight away about the money she had saved because she first had to check with the witness protection people to make sure they felt it was safe enough for me to have a holiday back home. She hadn't wanted to raise my hopes if they had then turned around and said it was too dangerous for me to come. Witness protection said that as Mum was now living in another state, it was safe for a time for me to return to Australia but they impressed on Mum that as few people as possible know of the trip and that we not venture into New South Wales, where Many was living.

I will never forget the feeling of exuberance on hearing the captain of the plane announce over the intercom that we had passed into Australian airspace. The trip had been a long one that took us via Singapore. Ben had been such a good little boy and not only was he looking forward to seeing his nanny for the first time, he was due to have a birthday while we were in Australia. Shawn had been wonderful about letting me take Ben with me for a month and had even helped organise Ben's visa. I knew Mum and Aunt Billie were going to be at the airport and I couldn't wait to see their faces. It was going to be one hell of a homecoming. I couldn't get off the plane fast enough.

At the same time, I felt great apprehension about returning to Australia. I wondered what I was coming back to. I could not shake my fears although I did long for the sense of security being back with my family would give me. When the captain announced we were beginning our descent into Brisbane, I craned my neck to look out of the left of the plane where I could see the airport. I started to cry and turned to my beautiful little boy. I held him close and told him: 'We're home, Ben, we're really home.'

The moment the wheels of the plane touched down, I started gathering all our things together off the floor and out of the seat pocket. The plane seemed to take forever to taxi to the terminal. As soon as we could get off the plane, I grabbed Ben, raced into the terminal and handed my passport to the man at the immigration counter. He looked at the passport, then back at me, then back at the passport and then asked me to stand aside while they checked it. To this day I have no idea what the problem was but I was worried that something was wrong because it did not carry my real name. The ten minutes I waited seemed like an eternity. Finally the officer said everything was fine and I could go through. With a sigh of relief, I straightened up, brushed my hair and headed out to see my family.

The corridor that led out into the main terminal was very wide and the whole of the left side was glass. Behind it was a sea of faces. How on earth would I be able to find Mum and Aunt Billie? I looked for them among the crowd while trying to steer the luggage trolley and walk slowly enough for

Ben to keep up with me. I shouldn't have worried about finding them—at the end of the corridor was a small gate that opened automatically and standing right behind it were these two wonderful women making absolute spectacles of themselves. Mum and Aunt Billie stood right in front of everyone, waving five coloured balloons. Mum and I saw each other at the same time and by the time I reached the gate we were both crying. We held each other tightly, burying ourselves in each other's shoulders. Mum then turned to Ben, picked him up and twirled him around, sending him into fits of giggles. Then with all the innocence of a child, he muttered the word: 'Nanny.' It had us all laughing and crying at the same time. I was home.

My time in Australia flew by, filled with the hugs and laughter I had so missed. Mum and I spent almost every moment together, staying most weekends with Aunt Billie and Uncle Greg. It was like nothing had changed. We would all sit around together, holding hands and making the most of what little time we had. Ben had the most wonderful time. Not only was there his family but he was running around outside and doing all the things that neither space nor weather allow children to do in London. I started pondering the possibility of returning to Australia to live. There was the possibility that Shawn may not let me take Ben away with me to another country and there was no way I could afford an expensive custody battle. More worrying was Fred Many.

The police had been keeping a close watch on Many since he got out of gaol. They knew almost every move he had made. They knew that the day after he got out of gaol, he had headed straight up to the Central Coast looking for his ex-wife, Lyndie Cashman—and revenge. He was furious with her for telling police about the two armed robberies. He could not get to me because he did not know where I was but he could try to find her. He visited a couple of pubs where she was known, had a few drinks at the bar and casually asked where she lived. No-one would tell him. Thankfully he never found out her new surname.

Since then, the police had been watching him in Bathurst. They knew his visitors, many of them former fellow prisoners. His wife Barbara had fallen pregnant and almost nine months to the day he was released from prison, she had their baby. Her former husband, a plant operator who lived on the Central Coast with his second wife and two sons, made an application to the Family Court for custody of his two daughters when he learned they were living with Many. He sold his story to a women's magazine and branded Many a 'monster'. On the day the custody case was due to be heard, Barbara's ex-husband turned up at court and was met by police with outstanding criminal warrants for his arrest. The man's two daughters remained with Many.

Meanwhile a Sydney newspaper tracked Many down to Bathurst and splashed his picture across the front page. In an effort to disappear from the media and a disapproving public, Many then changed his name to Glen Harris, Glen being his middle name. But it was not going to be that easy for him to hide from public view. He was soon back in court, under his real name of Fred Many, charged with the two armed robberies committed while he had been free in 1986. He was released on bail but had to report daily to his local police station.

Mum and I had been kept up to date with what Many was doing both through the witness protection people and reporters, who still seemed to know more than the police. Before I was due to fly back to London, I met with Grahame from witness protection and discussed the possibility of me coming back to Australia to live. He felt I would still be taking a big risk by doing so but he could understand what a lonely time I was having being exiled to another country. His final verdict was that if I truly wanted to return to Australia for good, then they would find a way to help me do it and keep me safe.

When the time came to say goodbye at Brisbane's International Airport, it seemed as if it had been only yesterday that I had arrived. I was sure the pain I felt really was my heart breaking. I hated Many with every ounce of my body for making me leave my family yet again. I can remember muttering to my son as the plane neared London: 'Welcome back to yucky England, Ben.'

Shawn was at the airport to pick us up and take us to our new flat. While I had been away, the lease on my old flat had run out and with all the last minute preparations to go to Australia, I had not had the time to find somewhere new before I left. The choice of places to rent was limited but Shawn said he had found Ben and me another ground floor flat with two bedrooms. He said it needed some work done but wasn't too bad. When we pulled up in front of the building, it indeed looked quite nice. It was sur-rounded by well-tended gardens and appeared clean enough. It turned out that the outside was the best part of the place. The three of us walked up to the door of my flat and when Shawn opened the door I burst into tears. The flat was freezing cold and dirty. There were no carpets, only floorboards that were not properly sealed so the cold winter air blew up through them. The walls and wallpaper were yellow with age and the place smelled mouldy. I looked down at Ben and thought of the beautiful warm weather in Australia and the wonderful clean family home of Mum's and wondered how on earth I could do this to him. I felt like such a failure.

I headed into what would be my bedroom and put down my luggage. The only thing to do was to unpack everything and make the place as liveable as possible. Shawn had had all my furniture delivered, what little there was of it, and the fridge was turned on. At least I could make Ben a glass of warm milk to keep the chill off him.

I was able to make a reasonably nice home for Ben and yet I still longed to be back in Australia. One night I was sitting in the lounge room, Ben was in bed asleep and I thought about the situation I was in. How dare Fred Many be able to live his life as a free man while I was banished to England. I felt I had let things drift for too long and had to take control of my life. I had to reclaim it as my own. With that in mind, I went on to try to figure out a way of returning to Australia.

Tentatively, I brought it up with Shawn and to my surprise, he agreed to let me take Ben with me out of the country. He said he realised I could give Ben a better home and that the lifestyle in Australia would be much better for Ben. Now I needed the money to pay for our tickets. I remembered that

60 Minutes had promised a return ticket to London for Mum so she could come and visit me and it was an offer we had not taken up. We had been saving it for a rainy day. This was the rainy day. Once I had made up my mind what to do, I rang Mum one evening and told her of my plans. She was ecstatic. She didn't need to be asked twice to contact *60 Minutes* and ask if we could change the promised return ticket to two one-way tickets for Ben and me. Neither of us spoke about the consequences of me returning home. Mum realised I was determined enough to go through with it regardless of the threat from Many. By that time, no-one could stop me. *60 Minutes* agreed to change the tickets and I booked the flight. It turned out that the only seats available were on a flight that would land in Brisbane on Christmas morning. It was the perfect time to arrive home and I could not have picked it better myself. What a Christmas it turned out to be. Mum was at the airport to meet us but this time there were no tears. We knew we didn't have to say goodbye again.

I arrived back to my new life with just two suitcases. I had sold what little furniture I had in London and it gave me enough money for Ben and me to get by on. Mum was an absolute angel and together we worked on picking up the pieces of our lives. I had used my married name while in London and decided to stick with it now I was home because we figured it would make it even harder for anyone to track me down but we were still very careful about who knew I was back in the country. We told hardly anyone apart from family. Mum, Ben and I lived in the tiny one-bedroom flat Mum was renting in Brisbane. I wanted to get out and get a job so I could meet people and support Ben and myself financially, but it was difficult because I had left school at fifteen because of the attack. I had no qualifications and hadn't had the opportunity to do any further studies because of all that had happened since. I also had Ben to look after and he was having a ball being back in Australia with his family around.

I made the decision to leave Brisbane and return to the Central Coast to live. Needless to say, Mum and the rest of the family were horrified. Why on earth would I want to return to the area where everything had occurred? I explained that I refused to run and hide forever. If Many never went back to gaol, I did not want to spend the rest of my life living in a shadow world in a city where I didn't want to be and where no-one could know who I really was. I decided to be stubborn and not keep giving in to Fred Many. I felt it was time for me to face the memories. I was feeling much stronger being back home and being surrounded by the love and support of my family. I felt that every time I was cautious or fearful, I was feeding the actions of Fred Many. I wanted to see if I could get back the kind of life I felt I would have had if only I had not got in the car with him that day back in 1986. After many conversations with Mum during which she could see I was adamant, she agreed to travel with me to the Central Coast to find somewhere to live. Aunt Billie joined us on the trip.

I saw a beautiful house on the Coast, well away from Terrigal, and fell in love with it straight away. We all knew this was the house for Ben and me. I couldn't wait to move in and get to work on making it ours. It was full of light and such a far cry from the damp and dark ground floor flat where we were living in London. Ben had his own room and loved to play in there.

We had been in contact with the witness protection people since I returned to Australia and had been assigned a new officer to the case—but we didn't dare tell them I had moved back to the Central Coast. They didn't know I was living there—until one day, I suddenly needed them when I thought my worst nightmare had come true.

Despite my bravado, I had never fully relaxed back on the Coast. When I was out in the streets, I couldn't wait to get home. I made an effort to keep to myself and not draw any attention to me. I still had the odd panic attack when I thought that a car had been behind me for too long or that someone had been following me around the supermarket for a while. Of course they always turned out to be innocent events and I would yell at myself for being so silly and paranoid. The few old friends in the area I had been in touch with had been sworn to secrecy. One of them even went so far as to tape my telephone number under his coffee table so no-one would find it. Sounds extreme, I know, but I could not be too careful.

I found work as a receptionist in the legal office of a friend of mine and relished the fact I was earning a living again. Ben was thriving in pre-school and life seemed to be travelling well. Until I saw Fred Many.

One of my duties at work included collecting the mail every morning from the local post office. I had parked my car and was crossing the road when I passed a man. I just caught a glimpse of him but it stopped me dead. All I had seen of this man were his eyes but that was enough. I knew I had seen them before. I knew they were Fred Many's eyes. I had changed my looks considerably since my time in court and also since the *60 Minutes* interview but I couldn't help but feel scared and threatened. I raced to the post office where I knew there would be plenty of people. As I emptied the mailbox, I kept looking out into the street to see where he had gone but I couldn't see him, although there were few people about. I tried to convince myself that I was being silly, that it hadn't been him. But I knew my first instinct was right.

I ran back over the street to my car. I could have kicked myself because I'd left the doors unlocked. I checked the back seat to make sure no-one was hiding on the floor and even checked in the hatchback compartment. I never thought I would have to do that again and was amazed at how I was able to instinctively remember all the things John and Grahame had drummed into me about places to check. I drove like a mad woman back to work, checking along the streets to try to find the man I thought was Many and trying at the same time to make sure I wasn't being followed. As soon as I got back to work, I told my boss what had happened and she gave me the time I needed to organise things.

My first call was to Ben's pre-school where I asked them to keep a special eye on him and let me know if anyone went to the centre asking for him. I played on a story I had already made up about a custody battle with Ben's father. I had told them when Ben first started at the centre that under no circumstances was anyone other than myself allowed to pick him up. I had also asked that Ben not be used in any videos within the pre-school and even having his school photograph taken had worried me. If the pre-school thought I was completely paranoid and nuts before that day, my ringing them in a panic after seeing Many would only have reinforced their views. I didn't care.

The second call was made to John, but he was in a meeting. I rang Grahame, apologising because he was no longer with witness protection but I needed someone I could trust. I said I needed someone to find out exactly where Many was. I knew he was on bail for the armed robbery charges and had to report daily to his local police station. I hoped Grahame would be able to come back and tell me Many had already checked in with the police that morning. That would have put me at ease because he was living about a four-hour drive away which would have meant the man I saw wasn't Many. When Grahame called back he told me Many hadn't reported into the police as yet. I was mortified, I knew it really had been Fred Many who I had seen. Grahame told me not to panic, to stay calm and said he had asked witness protection to assign another officer to my case, someone I could talk to. He said she was called Melissa and reassured me that she was extremely good at what she did.

Before long, Melissa called. She said the police at the station to which Many was reporting had instructions to let her know the minute he reported in. Meanwhile, she and I spoke at length about my case. She gave me all the contact numbers for her and her partner in witness protection, Brad. She asked me why I hadn't told the witness protection team that I had moved into the house and I explained that I had wanted to try to get on with my life on my own, that I was trying to shake off the hold Many had on me. Melissa was very understanding. She suggested that she and Brad should visit me at home that evening.

That night, after I had safely picked Ben up from pre-school, Melissa and Brad arrived. She told me Many had reported to the police station late that afternoon. I told her I knew I sounded paranoid, but I was sure it was him I had seen. Melissa told me not to be too hard on myself and said I had every right to be feeling that way. She said it was possible he had been on the Coast that day. She showed me some shots of Many taken when he had been released from gaol and I explained that the man I had seen had appeared heavier than that. She said that he had indeed put on weight since the pictures had been taken. I found it very hard to look at the photographs, a fact Melissa picked up on and she quickly put them away. Before they left, they checked all the extra locks I had fitted to my house when I moved in and were happy with the security measures.

Since that night, I have spoken with Melissa regularly and found her support, professionalism and friendship to be very reassuring. I still have not been able to prove that the man I saw was Many but I believe that it was. I am also sure he did not recognise me, nor had he been looking for me. I was lucky that time.

With that day putting me back on full alert, my time back in the area has been a mix of good and bad. What I did not expect was to be surrounded with memories to the degree that I have been. For the first few months, every time I ventured out I was reminded of the day of the attack. The main road Many drove me along is the only road that leads through the area where I live. Every time I go to Sydney, I drive past the spot where I know that clearing in the bush is. I decided I had to face these reminders the best way I could. One day I asked a friend to look after Ben for me so I could have some time alone. No-one could do this for me, no-one could do it with me. I had to do it and I had to do it alone.

It was a cloudy, drizzling day on the day I travelled the same route Many had taken me that afternoon. I set out at 8.30 a.m. and headed first for the hill at Terrigal where I had walked up from the beach. From there, I continued on along the roads he had taken me, stopping at all the areas where he had stopped and finally ending up on the old highway. It was like driving through a time warp. Although everything was physically so different around me, the memories of that day in 1986 were crystal clear. I had a mixture of feelings as I retraced the journey; some of hatred, some of sadness and some of guilt. The surprising thing was that I was finally able to put it behind me. It was at that clearing in the bush that it all became clear to me.

It took me a while to find the spot because the whole area had changed when the freeway was built. Along the old highway there were factories where a lot of bush had been. Where the dirt track had been was now a narrow tarred road. I pulled into the road and switched off the engine. The place was silent. Not a soul was around. I sat in the car, looking at how different the scene now was. The track had been tarred for about ten metres in from the road and a six-foot wire fence built across it. There were gates, chained and padlocked. On the gates was the name of a local business and I realised this was now their land. It looked like a quarry.

The fence on either side of the gates went for only three metres and then stopped. I could see the tyre tracks of heavy vehicles in the dirt on the other side. Tentatively getting out of the car, I walked along the fence line and around the last pole holding up the fence and ventured into the scrub. I stood still while visions of the area as it had originally been came into my mind. The smell of the bush made it easy for me to be right back there, back on the day of the attack when I was fifteen. The bush plants all around looked familiar. I shook my shoulders to break the spell and took some steps towards ending this period of my life.

I walked along the track, the digging that had been going on had disguised the area and I lost my bearings. I stepped off the track into the bush to look for the clearing where I had been taken and was able to make out a car wreck under some scrub. My immediate thought was that this was it, this was the burnt-out car. As I got closer, I saw it was a very old Dodge truck. Standing there looking at the truck, I realised I had been holding my breath. Taking a lungful of the bush air, I pressed on. I could not find what I was looking for so I retraced my steps and headed into another area of scrub. I climbed up a steep embankment and tried to get my bearings. I knew I had to be very close to the clearing because I was certain it had been roughly this distance away from the track. I came to the top of the embankment and looked around but nothing looked familiar. It became very confusing. I had been there about half an hour by this time, wandering in all directions. I saw more car wrecks, but none of them was the same one that I remembered so clearly from 1986. I headed back to the gates, deciding the best thing I could do was to start again with a better understanding of where the clearing might be.

From the gates, I walked directly along the track again, far enough to be sure I had reached where the clearing should have been. I turned right and headed straight out into the bush. I came upon a huge mound of dirt, which must have been bulldozed to the side when the track was widened. I walked around it and over it. Yes, it was about the right size and I realised the clearing and quite probably the wrecked car had been completely buried beneath the dirt. I sat down in the dirt and looked around. It sounds strange but I felt as if I was at a gravesite. The place that had for so many years held the secret of what had happened there had been buried and in that burial, I felt it had been purified. The car and the marks in the dirt which had been left by my struggle with Fred Many had disappeared under tonnes of dirt, never to be seen again. I just sat there for quite some time, looked and thought.

When I was ready, I stood up and as I dusted the dirt from my jeans, I felt I was dusting away the memories that this place had held for me for so many years. The people who now worked in this area had no idea what had gone on here. My innocence had been buried right here and I mourned for that. I drove away feeling I had said goodbye to part of the little girl I had once been. I was grateful the area had changed so much, it helped me accept that I had to change as well. I haven't been back there. I don't need to go back. A few nights after my visit, I had a dream in which I saw myself as a little girl again, struggling to crawl out from under the dirt. In my dream, I forced her back down and told her that I loved her. I awoke from that dream in tears but had to realise that I would never again be that little girl and so had to let her go.

Fred Many was back in the news. He had tried to have his trial on the two armed robbery charges put off, claiming he could never get a fair trial because of the adverse publicity that had surrounded him. The NSW District Court refused his application with the judge saying it was by then 1997 and there had been nothing written about him since 1995. Many tried an appeal to the NSW Court of Criminal Appeal but the winning streak that had helped him all those years ago had well and truly deserted him. His appeal was refused and he was due to face court again on 25 September 1997, when a new date would be set for his trial.

Janet Fife-Yeomans and I had become good friends and talked about writing this book together. I was a little unsure at first but after talking about it with a few friends and family, I felt the time had come to pull the whole story together and to try to look for some answers. Obviously I considered my safety and the safety of Ben and Mum but I felt that as my identity and my whereabouts would remain a secret, our safety could be protected. I gave up my job to concentrate on writing. I had become involved with a wonderful man, Patrick, who accepted my history and supported me through all the emotions that writing this book brought to the surface.

Something happened that changed my world again.

On the morning of Sunday, 21 September 1997, Janet rang me at home. She said: 'He's dead, Kir.' Fred Many had died. I stood in the kitchen with the phone to my ear and said nothing. I couldn't believe what I had heard. Many had moved from Bathurst to a Housing Commission flat in Sydney's western suburbs. He and Barbara had been having rows and they had recently separated, however he was back at their flat on the Friday night sitting in the lounge room watching TV while their baby and her two daughters were in bed. Janet told me he had complained of chest pains and numbness in his right arm earlier that day—the classic warning signs of a heart attack—but did not seek medical help. On the Friday night he collapsed and was dead by the time the ambulance arrived. There had been six days to go until he was due back in court to hear when his trial would be dealt with. He had died of a heart attack. He was forty-three.

Janet could sense I was in shock and said she would speak to me later in the day. I hung up the phone with a shaking hand and sat down in the lounge room, trying to take it all in. I didn't know how I felt. For so many years I had feared and hated this man, the man who had altered my life so dramatically, and now he was gone, just like that. It was too simple to believe. I waited a few minutes before phoning Mum and telling her the news. Her reaction was pretty much the same as mine. She found it hard to believe that it was all over. We had both been living lives of secrecy for so long that the prospect of being able to have our own lives back and live openly again was hard to accept.

We looked upon the news of Fred Many's death with the same caution we had been conditioned to living with for years. Was it real? I had been told it had happened and I saw it and heard it on the news the next morning. I read it in the papers but I still wasn't totally convinced. There had been so much uncertainty in our lives, how could we be certain of this?

I felt I had to speak with the Witness Protection Group before I could totally believe I was free of the past but before I had a chance, the phone rang early the next morning. It was Grahame. He had just heard the morning news and wanted to let me know what had happened. I explained I already knew. He went on to say how happy I must be. This was something so many people, both family and close friends, would say in the following days. I explained to Grahame that I really didn't know how I felt. I couldn't feel elation or pleasure at anyone's death, even Many's. He had left behind a wife and child and I felt for the both of them. Neither of them had asked for this just as I hadn't. I asked Grahame if he felt Mum and I were jumping the gun a little by thinking it was all over. He said we had every right to feel that way.

I could not get excited. I still had a nagging feeling that something would happen to shatter the feeling of closure and that something to do with the case would flare up and Mum and I would be thrown into mayhem again. I spoke to Melissa from witness protection and told her of my fears and my disbelief. She said in a firm, friendly voice that it was all over and that I had every right to scream from the top of a hill that I was now free of the shackles of the past. She said I should be out with friends having a celebratory drink. I was starting to feel that maybe it was all true and that I had indeed been given my life back.

I wanted to do something outrageous, something I would never have done just twenty-four hours earlier. There was a service station nearby which I used regularly and I went down there to get some milk. I had got to know Chris, who worked the morning shift, quite well but he had no idea of my past. That morning when I walked into the service station, I noticed a pile of newspapers with a photo of Many and the story of his death on the front page. This was it, this was the first step to losing the cloak of secrecy. I looked up at Chris and pointed to the story and said: 'That's me.'

It was a silly thing to do but for me it was such a big step to finally be able to tell people who I really am. I know it isn't something to boast about and I do not mean it in that way, but it is important to have that choice again. I had been given back the ability to make choices without having to ask others what they think, or even having to ask their permission.

To say Chris was surprised was an understatement but he was genuinely happy for me and told me to keep smiling and get on with my life. The next big step was my neighbours. Since moving to the house, I had been living like a hermit. The neighbours in my street are a lovely bunch of people and very friendly towards each other. One family invited most of the neighbours over to their house for a Christmas drink and a New Year's Eve drink. For the two years I had been there, they had also invited me but each year I stayed inside with my doors locked and quietly watched TV. I always felt dreadful but I knew that if I went I would have to face the usual questions about where I was from and about my past; the sort of things most people would ask a new neighbour and the things I couldn't truthfully answer. I couldn't face having to spin another web of lies.

With the need for secrecy gone along with Many's death, I started waving and saying hello to my neighbours. I didn't jump in wholeheartedly, that would have seemed odd, but I started chatting to them. One day before I knew it, I had told one of them about the case and why I had been keeping to myself. I was so surprised when they said they had already had some idea that something like that had been going on because they had recognised the cars that often pulled up outside my house as unmarked police cars. I haven't spoken about it with them all, but I know that by now they have accepted that I had my reasons for keeping away. It may sound like a small step to speak to a neighbour, but for me it was very significant.

Others involved in this tale reacted to Fred Many's death in different ways. John Davidson said that the only thing that might be said in favour of Many was that 'at the end of his worthless life, he at least provided employment for someone to bury him'. Tom Domican said he bore no grudge against his accuser but said his death was the best thing that could happen 'for the children in the community'. But right to the end, Fred Many not only showed no remorse for what he had done but continued to spin his fairytales and to do it convincingly. One of the three Legal Aid solicitors who had been representing him on the armed robbery charges told a reporter that he was not convinced Many was guilty of attacking me. When confronted with the evidence, including the fingernails in the boot, the solicitor said: 'Well, he never denied he had a relationship with the girl.'

I have been proud that by standing up and fighting, by drawing attention to what Many got away with, Mum and I have in some small way helped to make the justice system fairer. Not only did Many never give evidence in a court again, but also his fiasco signalled the end of prison informers and the industry they had become in the mid-1980s. Since then, they have not been used as widely. Now there has to be independent evidence to support their story. The publicity given to cases like Many's has also meant the police have to keep a central register of all informers, in prison or otherwise. It means that it should, in theory, be easier to test their motives because so much about the rewards of informing is no longer so secret.

For me, the most important thing to come out of this so far as the legal system is concerned is that informers who lie can have any sentence reduction snatched back. Where would Fred Many be today if that had happened? Back in gaol and probably still alive.

I hope the justice system will never again be able to break down like it did. Fred Many was able to make the police, the courts and the New South Wales Government look like fools. There is no doubt he was cunning but in his favour was that the system he so successfully manipulated was ready to be used and wide open for abuse. The lies he spun at the beginning were messy to untangle because he was informing both for the New South Wales Police and the National Crime Authority, traditional rivals. The mess continued as one hand never knew what the other was doing—one set of judges did not know what another set had already done. As Many himself said in the statement he released from gaol on the eve of walking free in 1995: 'If (I have) benefited by an inadequate system, it is the system that needs changing (as it has been).' He could say that because by then it was too late. He had beaten that system.

While he died with the armed robbery charges hanging over him, he was never to be charged with the perjury and conspiracy to pervert the course of justice over Peter Bruce's 'rescue' at Goulburn Gaol. I also wonder why it is that the people who gave evidence at the trial on behalf of Many, and lied, were never charged with perjury or reprimanded in any way. I am not on a crusade or acting out of some feeling of vendetta, I'm just asking the simple questions most people would. More significantly, Fred Many was never charged with threatening to kill Mum and me by placing the murder contract on our lives. When Many was released from gaol, the NCA denied in the media that there was ever a tape recording of the telephone call from gaol, despite what they told us back in 1987. I have spoken to an officer involved at the time and he told me there was indeed a tape of that call but that he had been told it has since been destroyed. There had also been written transcripts which included the name of a corrupt police officer who had been mentioned as being able to help find Mum and me. The threat was serious enough to change the direction of our lives and place us in protection with all that entailed. Yet from what we have been able to learn, no-one named in that telephone call has been questioned about it. This threat from Many turned out to be the sole reason for the drastic change in our lives, more, much more, than the rape itself, yet no-one has been charged over it. Why?

While his death has given me my life back, I'm not sure if I will ever be able to get my real name back but I'm trying. My birth name is the one on the cover of this book yet officially, I no longer exist anywhere by that name. My birth certificate, driver's licence, passport, bank accounts, title deeds to my house and bills are all in a different name. When I was married in England, it was even under my new identity.

I would be lying to myself if I said I didn't feel bitter about the past twelve years. Fred Many put myself and my family through hell yet was able to regain his freedom some twelve years early and then was able to fend off any future prosecution by his untimely death. I do feel cheated that he no longer has to live with what he did while I do. I have put the worst behind me, but the memories still linger.

But don't pity me and don't feel sorry for me. I have come out of this a much stronger person than I could ever have imagined. I take time every day to appreciate that I am here. I want people to remember me for my strength and not remember me as 'Fred Many's victim'. I'm not his victim any longer.